Reclaiming a Christian Moral Compass

Reclaiming a Christian Moral Compass

Living in anticipation and preparation for Jesus' promised return as the Righteous Judge is — OUR ONLY HOPE!

THOMAS FITZHUGH SHEETS

ReadersMagnet, LLC

Reclaiming A Christian Moral Compass: Living in anticipation and preparation for Jesus' promised return as the Righteous Judge is — OUR ONLY HOPE!
Copyright © 2024 by Thomas Fitzhugh Sheets

Published in the United States of America

Library of Congress Control Number: 2024918030
ISBN　　Paperback:　　979-8-89091-711-9
ISBN　　eBook:　　979-8-89091-712-6

All rights reserved. No part of this publication may be reproduced, stored in a retrieval system or transmitted in any way by any means, electronic, mechanical, photocopy, recording or otherwise without the prior permission of the author except as provided by USA copyright law.

The opinions expressed by the author are not necessarily those of ReadersMagnet, LLC.

ReadersMagnet, LLC
10620 Treena Street, Suite 230 | San Diego, California, 92131 USA
1.619. 354. 2643 | www.readersmagnet.com

Book design copyright © 2024 by ReadersMagnet, LLC. All rights reserved.

Cover design by Tifanny Curaza
Interior design by Dorothy Lee

PART 1: CHRISTIAN LABEL OR LIFESTYLE

Foreword 7
Chapter #1 - The Rebellion 14
Chapter #2 - The Exodus Connection 18
Chapter #3 - The Gospel According to Paul 20
Chapter #4 - Dying for The Kingdom 23
Chapter #5 - My Four and No More 28
Chapter #6 - Becoming Worthy of Our Calling 31
Chapter #7 - Dullness of Mind 37
Chapter #8 - Storge Love 40
Chapter #9 - The Family of God 44
Chapter #10 - The Calvinized Christian Culture 50
Chapter #11 - The I Never Knew You Crowd 55
Chapter #12 - The Jesus that I Know 58
Chapter #13 - The Collaboration Leading to the Destination 63
Part 2: Reclaiming A Christian Moral Compass 67
Part 3: God Uses Who He Chooses 80
Author Biography 87

FOREWORD

I first titled this book "The Rebellion" based on what Jesus teaches us in The Parable of The Minas in Luke 19. Starting at verse 11, "While they were listening to this, he went on to tell them a parable, because he was near Jerusalem and the people thought that the kingdom of God was going to appear at once." Jesus is focused here on the instant gratification crowd, His going away and His return as the Righteous Judge. If you can, please read this parable now for yourself before you continue. This was the motivation for me to continue to write and help the instant gratification crowd see that belief gets us to Judgment but lordship and obedience, to all He commands, gets us through Judgment.

We can pass on to our children, by teaching and by example, a faith that ignores the reality of Final Judgment or a faith that prepares them for that event. In either case, God's love and how we experience that love is at stake and how youthful - immature minds handle those two very different views. We can instill in them a sense of entitlement to a heavenly reward at their death or, much better, a devoted affection that is shared in The Family of God as they journey to that promised Day of reward. Not locked in a prison of entitlement, but looking forward to a promotion, or maybe a diploma, or just maybe a pure gift for having lived a life that pleases God. At Jesus' return, He establishes His Kingdom right here on this earth. Our welcome into The Kingdom will be dependent on our lifestyle and The Godly Family Values we passed on to the next generation.

This book is based on the Gospel Paul preached that begins with the first forty-eight verses of Romans as he adds to it throughout his letters. Paul's faith, The Faith of the First-Century Church, was in Jesus' promise to return bringing salvation with Him. We are perfected in that faith. Today we have a faithless generation with the label of Christian but mostly, or maybe often, living disobedient lifestyles. They live in a world of entitlement and entertainment having been taught to believe that salvation is freely given at the moment of belief and that lifestyle doesn't matter and has no connection to their eternal reward. At Jesus' return, He rescues the obedient as God's wrath is poured out on the disobedient.

What is missing in many of our families and churches and in our country is a strong moral compass that always points to true north, that is The One who is The Truth - Jesus. Postmodern theologians pride themselves on not knowing the truth and what truth is and then want to pass that ignorance on to the next generation. A generation without truth is a generation without a moral compass. A morally impure spirit is filling that vacuum and is invading our families, our churches and our country and may explain the wilderness we find ourselves in today.

John Wesley, my modern hero of the faith, lived at the same time that our country's government was being formed. He warned that the theology of The Church of England would lead to lawlessness and the moral decay of that culture. At the time there was only one culture in England, the church culture. George Washington warned that this new government would only work for a moral people. Both men were prophets of their time, concerned about living in a future world without a Christian Moral Compass.

We now have a president who inherited a secure southern border that needed to be finished. He opened that border up to all comers and created an ongoing crisis, hoping to transform America, starting with an all-out assault on the American Economy. He said recently that his desire was to "fundamentally transform our economy". This echoes his former boss's statement right before he took office, "We are five days away from the fundamental transformation of America". There is much evidence that this invasion of millions of illegals across our southern border would play an important part in their plan of transforming this country into a socialist nation and thus destroy The American Dream.

This transformation has been happening before our very eyes. Example: the transformation from four years of relative peace and prosperity to four years of crisis - after crisis - after crisis. In spite of a plandemic, deadly riots and over four years of trying to overthrow a duly elected president, their insurrection has failed, but they keep trying. With the help of the main stream media helping to hide their agenda, we are told that the former president is the source of the problem and dangerous. The real danger can be seen in sanctuary cities where those who want to live The American Dream are now imprisoned by lawless people in the streets, led by those who want the socialist/entitlement dream of utopia to come true.

These Wolves in Sheep's Clothing come to kill and destroy using fear and hatred with the promise that they will build back better (socialist) what they mean to destroy. Their fruit is a promise to build their utopia on top of these ashes. But first, using the legal system, they must destroy the MAGA MAN who speaks truth to power and promises to lead and MAKE AMERICA GREAT AGAIN. They project their destructive agenda and the problems they create on to him and his supporters and then "deny-deny-deny" and "never let a crisis go to waste". This is community organizing 101 at its best and, if allowed to continue, will lead to a world crisis of biblical proportions. Watch out for Shrink-Flation - shrinking the food supply while increasing the money supply which they will blame on everyone but themselves.

It is obvious that a country founded by men who loved God, who wanted to put the power of government into the hands of the American People, is now run by men who love power and money. They have a very different agenda. They have the moral compass of those who caused two world wars. Character assassination, chaos, poverty and the premature death of millions of people is necessary for them to achieve their goals. They are determined to destroy the American Dream and return to a time where those with power and money ruled the world.

Wag The Dog

We have three great examples of this shift in power going on in our court system today. A local district attorney in Atlanta, Georgia is doing her very best to end the political carrier of Donald Trump. She has shown us that cash-money and power rule her life. At the same time, we have The Attorney General of New York State, who pledged to voters to get Trump, doing the same thing using her power and a lot more money. And then we have The President and The Senate telling The House of Representatives that the world will end if they don't pass a multi-billion-dollar emergency spending bill. How dare they go home to their voters and find out what their constituents want before they vote. Beware of those in congress who claim to want to fix the problem but will help keep leaders in power who are the problem.

Donald Trump's popularity continues to grow as this diabolical scheming is revealed. Trying to kick him to the curb will be their undoing as voters across this land find that they have the power and can kick these bullies to the curb instead. Donald Trump has had a target on his back since at least 2015 and seems to be ready to spend his last cent to put the people, who made this country great, back in power where they belong. It would be stupid for the The New York State A. G. to bite the hand that feeds her state unless she is doing it for the one who has the power to write her a blank check and replace that lost revenue. If you think this is just stupidity, you are part of the "useful idiot crowd" that helps these people stay in power.

At first, in the founding of this country, the people had the the freedom to vote in two federal elections. Every two years, they voted for a person to represent them in The House of Representatives who had the power of the purse (tax, spend and borrow). Every four years they had the freedom to vote for President, a person who had the power protect them from foreign invasion but did not have the power to tax them. They did not elect Senators, they were appointed by the governors of each state to protect the states from the federal government that might become too powerful and also to protect a minority of states from the majority. This worked very well accept for one thing that threatened the plan from the very beginning - Slavery.

The Democrat Party of The South and The Republican Party of The North went to war which threatened to destroy what the founding fathers had put into place. That issue is still being used and still threatens the survival of this nation, maybe more so now than at any time in our short history. Reigniting the flames of a past war when the Democrat Party lost the 2016 Presidential election seems to have worked well for them. It is coming to light that they hate America as it was founded and also hate the Europeans who, they say, invaded this land including many other parts of the world.

Many of those coming to this new land, sought freedom from religious wars and persecution, some escaping with their very lives. This land of the free and home of the brave is becoming a very dangerous place because of lawlessness and moral decay and another invasion. Those first Southern Democrats did not want to destroy this nation, they just wanted to be left alone to live a life that was immoral to many others in this country.

That conflict has been hijacked by those who do want to destroy this country, as it was founded, a nation with a Christian Moral Center. Do they want to replace it with communism or socialism? Maybe, but I think not. With what has happened recently on our university campuses and the middle east, I fear Islamic jihad. They all have the same moral compass and celebrate the shedding of innocent blood from the womb to the tomb.

What we are witnessing today is the final stages of a movement to shift the power that was vested in the people of this land into The Senate and The Oval Office. We have witnessed the confrontation between the governor of Texas and The President. This has been Barack Obama's third term in The Oval Office. The Senate has become his resource of useful idiots. Mainly using The Senate to produce massive spending bills in His first two terms, he added $10 trillion to the national debt, doubling it to $20 Trillion.

The plandemic kept that ball rolling while The Democrat controlled Congress tried to overthrow the election of Donald Trump all the while adding another $14 trillion in debt. This and trying to keep a shell of a man in The Oval Office is not an America First agenda. It does, however, show their agenda and determination to keep their power, by any means possible, and away from The American People and them choosing Donald Trump to return to the Oval Office. It looks like Michelle Obama will be their candidate and, it that comes true and if elected, it will be her husband's fourth term in the Oval Office.

They are deathly afraid that all the things they have done to destroy this country, as it was founded, will be revealed. Abandoning Bagram Air Force Base was actually abandoning The Afghan People and invited the invasion of Ukraine. Abandoning the policy of starving Iran of petro dollars abandoned The Israeli People. Abandoning a secure southern border to a policy of an open border abandoned The American People's hope for a secure and peaceful future. All of this and more was designed to add to the debt and destroy our economy. In spite of their efforts to destroy ours and a free world economy, it just keeps chugging along but with a result that the rich get richer and the poor get poorer.

Bonus Question: How do we pay off a $35 trillion debt? Easy - Drill, Baby, Drill. Destroy Iran's ability to produce oil and then sell all our new production to China. Then, let The American People decide how to spend all that money in The People's House, don't start any more wars and watch as peace and prosperity break out all over the world. God uses who He chooses, Thank You, Jesus.

DON'T BELEIVE YOUR LYING EYES

"Nothing in all creation is hidden from God's sight. Everything is uncovered and laid bare before the eyes of Him to whom we must give an account.", Hebrews 4:13.

CHAPTER #1
The Rebellion

The purpose of this book is to bring all that I have written into focus on one thing; that is the rebellion of The Church against The Second Coming of Jesus. When evangelists do not mention the coming of The Righteous Judge in their salvation messages, they distort God's Plan of Salvation to the point of no return. The true meaning of sin is rebellion against God. Thus this omission of the predetermined meeting between God and man is a rebellion against God and creates institutionalized sin in The Church.

Jesus makes this point dramatically in the Parable of the Minas beginning at Luke 19:11. This has far reaching consequences for the culture both inside The Church and in the culture at large. A morally impure spirit has, for the most part, replaced The Holy Spirit in our churches and has taken charge of government institutions and institutions of higher learning. Satan, the prince of this world and high priest of the disobedient, has so confused the culture over what is good and what is evil, that it is hard to find the difference and the Light of the World can hardly be noticed in the darkness.

The idea that being saved is the first thing that happens in the Christian Life has its roots in Calvinism. This is now labeled Post Modern Gospel or post modernity and gives credit to The Holy Spirit for our salvation. Man is helpless to come to the saving knowledge of Jesus Christ without a divine appointment – The Holy Spirit comes into us and enables us to believe and at that very moment we are saved. This is incredibly naive as God is given credit for choosing who will be saved and who will not be saved from the beginning of time. For those who are not chosen, God becomes a heartless god and incredibly, dooms those lost souls to eternal separation from Him.

The spirit of that divine appointment does not remove man's desire to sin, the sin nature. Thus the sin nature continues to battle with the need "to obey all that I have commanded you." This morally impure spirit tells us that we are saved but our sinful behavior would or could continue. Those who preach and teach this dogma do not understand the complete work of The Cross. The flesh is crucified but The Spirit remains. Full commitment and willful obedience under the authority of God's commands brings freedom from this double mindedness.

Our sin nature is crucified with Christ and The Holy Spirit keeps us safe from the desire to sin. The double mindedness of the knowledge of good and evil is replaced with the knowledge of God when our flesh is crucified with Christ. Jesus puts this double mindedness on display on the way to The Cross. He prays, "Father, if you are willing, take this cup from me; yet not my will, but yours be done." Obedience to the Father's will is at stake. Double mindedness must be crucified and single minded obedience to The Father wins the day.

Jesus gives us a very detailed idea of the work of the Holy Spirit in the age of grace. In John 16:5-16, Jesus gives us insight into The Holy Spirit's work and the idea of salvation at the moment of belief is not there, but the idea of The Holy Spirit convicting us of guilt and sin, righteousness and Judgment is there. The Holy Spirit is leading us to make the decision to follow Jesus with single minded commitment and unconditional surrender, *"because those who are led by the Spirit are sons of God."*

Post modernity is, for all practical purposes, Calvinism 2.0, but is not taught as such. What is taught is a muddled mess emphasizing church life with all beliefs accepted about who

Jesus was and is today with no understanding of who He is going to be when He comes back. All beliefs are to be accepted without debate. In this culture, teaching and preaching are not used as tools to promote unity of The faith (one faith) or The Blessed Hope (one hope) as Paul describes in Ephesians 4. Instead, emphasizing and promoting The Church is all there is left to do and, of course, cleaning up the mess that this fog has created in our lives and in our churches.

Jesus is many things to many people, but one thing remains the same – from Genesis to Revelation He is The Righteous Judge. *"...There will be a time of distress such as has not happened from the beginning of nations until then. But at that time your people – everyone whose name is found written in the book – will be delivered. Multitudes who sleep in the dust of the earth will awake; some to everlasting life, others to shame and everlasting contempt."* Daniel 12;1-2. This is a prophesy of The Second Coming and is not fulfilled until that event.

Jesus echoes this prophesy in John 5:28-29, *"Do not be amazed at this, for a time is coming when all who are in their graves will hear his voice and come out - those who have done good will rise to live, and those who have done evil will rise to be condemned."* Note here that Jesus refers to Himself in the third person, not "my voice" but "his voice" – the voice of The Righteous Judge.

The Promise of resurrection comes to all, but The Promise of life in The Kingdom is reserved for those who have obeyed and been productive for The Kingdom. Man is judged by what was done with what he was given. The Son of Man comes to reward the faithful – not as a worker earning his pay. But as a promised reward like a man pursuing the woman of his dreams. Grace must be understood as this promised reward of a love relationship and being part of The Family of God – not as a free gift without strings, but as a bonus for a life lived well and a dream come true.

Salvation is never more than a promise in this mortal life. Man goes from living in The Promise – to living in the Kingdom "on that Day". The gift of grace is received at the moment of conversion when man's mortal life becomes a spiritual life, begotten by God and serving Him eternally. Salvation should be seen as a bonus for loving and living in The Family of God with the promise of a future resurrection. Any other idea is rebellion against God and that is SIN. The focus should be on losing your life for the Kingdom. *"...but whoever will lose his life for me will save it."*, Luke 9:24.

CHAPTER #2
The Exodus Connection

It is not easy to see the parallel between the story in The Parable of the Minas and Moses coming down the mountain with God's instructions – The Ten Commandments. Moses comes down the mountain the first time with the word of the Lord saying, "So Moses went down to the people and told them. And God spoke all these words: ..." Jesus is that "word made flesh", The Covenant. Much later Moses, having gone back up the mountain, comes back down to a morally impure people who needed correction. Upon seeing this and the Golden Calf, Moses shatters the tablets on which God had written The Testimony (or maybe The Promise) – inscribed by the finger of God.

Paul writes that Jesus will come back to an apostate church – a church with a morally impure spirit without understanding and in need of correction but, by then, it's too late. Both stories here, in Exodus and the Minas, portray an angry God (king) wanting to kill all those who have disobeyed. Later in Exodus 34 with Moses again on the mountain, God has Moses chisel out two more tablets on which God writes the words that were on the first two tablets – The Testimony. Then in short order, God instructs Moses to write out the words of The Covenant on two more tablets – The Ten Commandments. Seems like there were two sets of tablets – one The Testimony inscribed by the finger of God and the other – The Covenant - The Ten Commandments – inscribed by Moses.

God put this connection in my head as I was writing "The Land of The Promise" and it is worth repeating. The lawlessness and moral decay in our world is so apparent and the Golden Calf represents the love of money (the root of all evil) and disobeying God's Law. It may be that the apostate church is today's Golden Calf. Reading through this passage in Exodus is most informative. From chapter 19 to 34 we go from the people agreeing to obey The Covenant, to the word of mouth delivery of The Ten Commandments, to Moses actually inscribing them on tablets of stone.

Moses comes down from the mountain twice with two tablets inscribed by God with The Testimony. I like to think that The Testimony is The Promise of a promised land God made to His Chosen People. The Promise which Paul shares with us in the first three chapters of Galatians vividly including, "If you belong to Christ, you are Abraham's seed and heirs according to The Promise". The shattered tablets in front of The Golden Calf represents the breaking of The Promise by not living in obedience to God's instructions.

To get the same message across, I used the image of a broken arrow on the cover of my book, "The Death of The Promise". At that time, I had not made the connection that I am making now. Moses was a long time coming and while he was gone, God's Chosen People chose to rebel in sin and disobedience – not unlike what is going on in the Church Culture today. The God of the Bible is The Righteous Judge from beginning to end and the God of the obedient – Satan is the god of the disobedient who will come under judgment at the Last Day.

Chapter #3
The Gospel According to Paul

Paul begins his letter to the Galatians with a warning – to preach a different gospel than the one he preached would bring on eternal condemnation. He preached that we are justified by faith, saved by grace through that faith with the hope of eternal life. His faith was in the awarding of salvation by The Righteous Judge – Jesus at Final Judgment. Post Modern Theology seeks to obscure this accounting at Jesus' return. It preaches belief in Jesus, that is the evidence of salvation and which is awarded at that moment of belief. Also, they preach that possessing eternal life is the first thing that happens at conversion. Paul preached that at the moment of conversion, we are saved from who we used to be and that we are new creatures with the hope of eternal life.

Recently, I was given a clear picture of this Post Modern Gospel in an item in our church bulletin titled "What is ADVENT – Advent means 'coming.' Since the early days of the church, Advent was celebrated because Jesus came to earth as a baby born in Bethlehem and because He will COME again as the risen Christ to rule triumphantly over life in heaven and earth." This is a prime example of that flawed theology. This is contrary to the return of Jesus as The Righteous Judge holding us accountable and ruling over Paradise here on this earth not in Heaven.

Looking at "Thy kingdom come, thy will be done on earth as it is in heaven." In The Sermon on the mount, we can see that Jesus is going to set up His Kingdom on this earth. He rules over a restored paradise here on earth having brought His Kingdom with Him as He returns. There is no separation of the righteous and unrighteous at their death. As in The Minas, The Sheep and The Goats and other parables they are separated (sorted) when The Righteous Judge returns.

Looking at "He's coming again to judge the quick and the dead." from The Apostle's Creed, Jesus returns as The Righteous Judge – for a final accounting for what we did with what we were given. At Christmas we celebrate the coming of Jesus as a baby born in Bethlehem who grows up to become the suffering servant – dying on a Roman cross to fulfill His calling at His First Advent. At His Second Advent, He returns as The Righteous Judge and to fulfil all that is associated with that event. At His Birth He is both servant and judge.

This example shows that the Post Modern Gospel is a far cry from the True Gospel of Jesus Christ – the Gospel Paul preached – *"Now there is in store for me the crown of righteousness, which the Lord, the righteous judge will award to me on that day – and not only to me, but also to all who long for his appearing."*, 2 Timothy 4:8. Again Paul warned us about the practice of preaching a gospel other than the one he preached – "let him be eternally condemned."

This false gospel is evident in all churches that I have experienced – so this false gospel must be being taught in most if not all evangelical seminaries today. If a graduate of seminary comes out with the belief that one is saved eternally at the end of the journey, not at the beginning, he or she will not find a job. Once again, this is evidence that today's church is in rebellion against The Second Coming and all that is associated with that future event – a church filled with the "I never knew you" crowd found in Matthew 7 – I'll get to that later.

I have met one preacher and believe there are many more who do not preach what they truly believe because they know they would lose their jobs if they did. Another example of post modernity is in teaching that Jesus "bore my cross". Jesus bore my sin as he died on His Cross. Post modernity doesn't like to talk about our sin. And of course salvation is fulfilled at The Second Coming and it is never free - it comes at the cost of our very lives.

Chapter #4
Dying for The Kingdom

The person that I deal with at my publisher complimented me on the cover of "on that Day". That got me to thinking about the composition of the picture and seeing it as symbolic of what the book is all about: I am standing on a state maintained gravel road that runs through my farm. That represents "The Road to Restoration" my first book. There is a barbed wire fence between me and the cows with the sky and Smith Mountain in the back ground; I can't get to the "Land of The Promise" because of the fence or boundary. I must travel that road of self-denial, daily picking up my cross, dying to myself and dying for The Kingdom in order to enter. There is a gate not too far from the picture that gives me access and is there to keep the cows in. Jesus says there is a narrow gate that few find. It is there to give us access to The Kingdom. It is well guarded and only the gate keeper has the key.

"Then he said to them all: "If anyone would come after me, he must deny himself and take up his cross daily and follow me. For whoever wants to save his life will lose it, but whoever will lose his life for me will save it." Luke 9:23-24. The contrast here is between living for yourself or dying to self and living for Jesus and His Kingdom. When I compare the similarities of the Parables of the Minas and the Talents, I find a contrast of joy and sorrow. Those who were productive for The Kingdom in The Talents are invited to join the king in his happiness. Those who rebel against the king's plan in the Minas experience a very

sorrowful event for all who are there – basically joining the king in his sorrow.

God has a word of encouragement for those who challenge the status quo in His Church: *"Blessed are you when people insult you, persecute you and falsely say all kinds of evil against you because of me. Rejoice and be glad, because great is your reward in heaven, for in the same way they persecuted the prophets who were before you."* Matthew 5:11-12. The idea that through our faithfulness we bring happiness to our God is lost on a generation that believes we are saved by grace alone. The joy of the moment of reward is lost in a world locked in a prison of entitlement.

The "do nothing gospel" revealed in The Talents and The Minas is in both parables. The one unit guys are reprimanded for doing nothing to the extent that by just putting their gift/money in the bank would have passively earned interest. The contempt that the king has for these two is monumental as well as their excuse making. The gift required no response in their minds and draws a perfect picture of today's cheap grace and a "do nothing gospel" which is so easy. This also reveals the paralysis of analysis of a double minded servant. It is in contrast to single minded service to the king and the joy and reward at Judgment.

These stories represent a very self-centered element in today's Christian Culture that is missing what may be the most important gift of all. The promise of a coming Judgment. It gives us a need to live our best life daily and to be worthy of that eternal reward at Jesus' return. What better gift can God give us than one we can pass on from generation to generation – that promise of reward and celebration at Final Judgment.

The writer of Hebrews identifies this unique faith in this promise in chapter eleven. If we read the first two verses followed by the last two verses here, this faith becomes clear. *"Now faith is being sure of what is hoped for and certain of what we do not see. This is what the ancients were commended for...*

These were all commended for their faith, yet none of them received what had been promised. God had planned something better for us so that only together with us would they be made perfect.", verses 1,2,39,40. Unity of faith in The Promise unites old and new and perfects all people in this faith in The Promise.

Being made perfect has to be about the absence of sin and the sin nature in the Kingdom and our election has the same properties. It seems that God thinks it is better for today's elect to live in The Promise rather than to live in a world where The Promise has already been fulfilled. The idea of man's unconditional election in post modernity needs to be replaced with man's unconditional surrender. Abraham was an example of this attitude, as was Moses, but today, we would rather focus on God's agape – charity/gift love and not on our love of God revealed in our unconditional surrender.

Early on, in one of my books, I identified Calvinists as the blame it on God group. This group disavows that there is a Final Judgment for believers by saying that they did nothing to earn salvation and need do nothing to keep it and with that logic, they are eternally secure. You will hear preachers say at times, "Just as man is destined to die once…, …to be absent from the body is to be present with the Lord." The instant gratification crowd have their scriptures; accept that this is what it actually there; *"So as there is Appointed to man once to die, (omitting, and after that this, Final Judgment.)",* Hebrews 9:27, The Pure Word. Then adding, "to be absent from the body is to be present with the Lord."

This comes from 2 Corinthians 5:8-10, *"We are confident, I say, and would prefer to be away from the body and at home with the Lord. So we make it our goal to please him, whether we are at home in the body or away from it. For we must all appear before the judgment seat of Christ, that each one may receive what is due him for the things done in the body, whether good or bad."* The instant gratification crowd has a way of taking a scripture that indicates salvation is earned by those who obey and is awarded at judgment and turning it so as to avoid judgment all together.

When it comes to eternal security the "do nothing gospel" taught and preached in today's churches is manifested in these two parables, The Minas and The Talents. The one unit guys receive their just reward at a judgment - a coming judgment that they, and today's Church Culture have ignored, and at the same time, disavowed. They will be sorry.

The picture of David and Goliath on the cover of my first book represents me taking on the whole Christian Culture. This was my thinking as I began to write and boy has it come true. It has been an adventure that I would not trade for anything. And would have never seen this connection without having gone through the process. God laid out His mission for me, and step-by-step, guided me, but it was for me to do. What a blessing!

So far, it seems that the main point that God has led me to make here is this: The instant gratification crowd has created their own plan of salvation which fails to mention and include Christ's Second Coming. Their plan is a counterfeit plan and thus a rebellion against God's plan. This rebellion is against God and fits the definition of SIN. This counterfeit plan takes advantage of man's fear of death and judgment which, in turn, puts leaders and followers of this plan into Satan's camp, *"...by his death (Jesus) he might destroy him who holds the power of death – that is the devil - and free all those who all their lives were held in slavery by their fear of death."*, Hebrews 2:14-15.

This is just another example of how a false message is being used to promote an agenda that is destroying The Church. Early in The Gospel of John, Jesus clears the temple and says this, *"Get these out of here! How dare you turn my Father's house into a market."*, John 2:16. Then His Disciples remembered this, *"Zeal for your house will consume me.'*, verse 17. In The Pure Word we find here, *"...has devoured me."*. The emphasis here on selling animals, especially doves, is about the blood sacrifice and rightly upset Jesus. Promoting a false gospel will have the effect of consuming – devouring The Family of God – The Body of Christ - The Church.

CHAPTER #5
My Four and No More

Around the age of forty God put into my brain the thought that my focus was to be on my neighbor – the person sitting next to me in church. Me learning about God and sharing that knowledge with others. While I was thinking about how to share this change in focus and write about it now, my wife found something that I had written, about that time, which I found to be life changing. At that time, I attributed my discontent and boredom with church to a lack of spiritual tension. The relationship between God and man needs the same elements as the tension that is in our human relationships. Movies and TV entertain using tension between good and evil. Sexual tension is probably used the most in today's entertainment and the main thing in tension is its value to make life interesting as well as entertaining.

Mysteries and sit-coms like "All in the Family" use tension to the utmost, but where are those elements in the church? Instant salvation and instant heaven have taken the tension out of our relationship with God and boredom has replaced the adventure. A raised hand has replaced the moment of surrender that brings us to our knees. Why buy the cow if you get the milk for free is an old adage but is as true in the church as anywhere else. "Salvation, freely given" leads to belief with no commitment. God's grace is in The Promise – our faith is in The Promise and single minded commitment should be our focus.

Loud music and repetitive lyrics have replaced the tension in church as entertainment and thus the church is at deaths door step. Belief with no commitment is sometimes translated as unbelief in Scripture. An example of this is in Hebrews 3:19, *"So we see that they were not able to enter, because of their unbelief."*, NIV – *"So we are Spiritually Seeing that they have not been made able to Enter because of no Commitment."*, The Pure Word. Here, belief with no commitment is the same as unbelief.

Perhaps the most important element of commitment is the commitment to tithe. It is a spiritual discipline but is seldom treated as such. Years ago, the church I was attending hired a consulting firm to help us raise funds to build a family life center. One of the things they said was, "Churches don't have financial problems, they have spiritual problems that are revealed in their finances." Of course the leaders of our church could not admit there was a spiritual problem, so nothing changed.

At times I would remind our leaders of that phrase until I was told not to say that any more. That frustration led to my wife and I leaving that church. We had been there for many years, at least 20. It was because of that advice that we became tithers and that was one of the best things we did as a family. It has been my experience that churches never treat their financial problems as a spiritual problem, to their demise.

Finding what I wrote years ago took me back to a moment in time that I had all most forgotten. My frustration had led me to a crisis of belief. While sitting through a finance committee meeting, I made a comment "there has to be a better way". I think I was at the point of leaving the church all together. Sometime later, I recalled that moment and my memory of that moment. I was walking around the room - like an out-of-body experience looking at myself from above. I decided that the Holy Spirit had placed His memory of that moment in my mind and then began to show me the better way.

My boredom and frustration was replaced by an adventure – discovering new and better ways to follow Jesus. That better way was about me sharing that adventure with my next-door-neighbor. It has been a journey into the unknown - leaving a known hell and finding an unknown glory. It was the first step in a journey – taking on the whole Christian Culture and writing about it.

CHAPTER #6
Becoming Worthy of Our Calling

Matthew 10 is a passage that connects being worthy of the reward at Final Judgment and devotion to the cause or for the purpose of The Way. *"I tell you the truth, it will be more bearable for Sodom and Gomorrah on the day (Day) of judgment (Final Judgment) for that town."*, verse 15. Here is The Promise, *"All men will hate you because of me, but he who stands firm to the end will be saved."* verse 22. Here is the cause. Start reading at verse 34 – ending at verse 39, *"...whoever loses his life for my sake (my cause) will find it."*, parallel reference Luke 9:23-24.

I find these two elements – being worthy and being devoted – so apparent in 2 Timothy 4:6-8 that it led me to put it in the name of my website (www.onthatday-timothy2468.com). This passage has become for me the summary of Paul's faith, the Gospel that he preached and God's plan of salvation – the end game. He was purified in waiting for Christ's return in his righteous acts of obedience. He attributes those same qualities to those who are also waiting and instructs teachers and preachers to bring the Body of Christ into the unity of that faith in The Second Coming, reference Ephesians 4.

In the Parable of the Minas, those who want instant gratification salvation and then rebel against The Second Coming turn the Day of the Lord into the day of death. This is the stark reality of Final Judgment. There is no middle ground, those who live preparing for the day judgment "on that Day" will receive eternal life, those who don't, will receive eternal death. This is the consequence of living in sin and disobedience, the sin nature.

I have created a new word to describe those who deny they are Calvinist but maintain that basic belief. They are "moderniacs", those who focus on instant salvation at the moment of belief and instant heaven at the moment they die, in the Calvinist tradition. It is forbidden to consider that salvation happens at the end of the journey which precludes the storybook ending which is portrayed in Scripture when Jesus comes back for His bride – The Church.

Looking forward to sexual fulfillment in marriage and all that comes with it is not unlike a similar spiritual purity we encounter in Scripture as we wait for The Soon Coming King. John Wesley connected the moral decay and lawlessness of his day to the theology of Calvinism and predestination. This lawlessness and moral decay has come true in our time resulting in the loss of salvation – The Promise of eternal life for the many traveling "The Broad Road". For those who live in The Promise, Jesus' return will be a promotion – for those who do not live in The Promise, His return will be a demotion. The kiss of death and eternal condemnation versus the kiss of resurrection and living in The Promise of Paradise.

A friend of mine claims to be a Hyper-Calvinist (5 point) and does not understand why I go to prison to share with those prisoners the Jesus that I know. He believes that a person is predestined to believe and needs only The Holy Spirit to move into their life – thus enabling them to believe and be saved. This is an example of the do-nothing gospel. He does not know the Jesus that I know. This is evidence of very seductive gospel that has been drilled into his head for years. This is in contrast to those first disciples who were called to be fishers of men. Fishermen do not just wait for the fish to jump into the boat.

In Galatians, Paul identifies a gospel other than the one he preached that leads to eternal condemnation which is actually no gospel at all. This is a problem that John, in 1 John 2, identifies, *"We know that we have come to know him if we obey his commands. The man who says, 'I know him,' but does not do what he commands is a liar, and truth is not in him. But if any one obeys his word, God's love is truly made complete in him. This is how we know we are in him."*, verses 3 and 4.

Warnings like this seem to be everywhere in the New Testament, but are not heeded by preachers today who define Jesus in every way accept as The Righteous Judge who is coming back. Do not be lead astray by people preaching a counterfeit gospel and a designer Jesus. In 1 John 2:28, John is promoting a life lived in anticipation and preparation for the coming of The Righteous Judge. *"And now, dear children, so that when he appears we may be confident and unashamed before him at his coming."*

What Paul writes in 2 Timothy 4:6-8 is so important and are words to live by. He feels he has done his very best to promote The Faith of The First-Century Church and has been obedient to his calling or mission. It is his faith in the promised coming of The Righteous Judge, it is the Gospel that he preached and it is the end game of God's Plan of Salvation all rolled up into three verses.

Hidden in Ephesians 4 we find Paul's Mission Statement to The Church. *"It was him who gave some to be apostles, some to be prophets, some to be evangelists, and some to be preachers and teachers, to prepare God's people for works of service, so that the body of Christ may be built up until we all reach unity in the faith and in the knowledge of the son of God and become mature, attaining to the whole measure of the fullness of Christ."* (Verses 11-13 NIV).

Key to understanding this mission statement is 'unity in the faith" which is faith in His return. Faith in His Second Coming, The Soon Coming King and The Righteous Judge is the glue that was to hold the Church together. Paul makes this point when he writes, *"From him the whole body, joined and held together by every supporting ligament, grows and builds itself up in love, as each part does its work."*, Ephesians 4:16.

Faith in a designer Jesus is the first step in creating the anti-Christ as sinful man defines for himself who Jesus is at any given time. It has become my mission to challenge The Church Universal to make Paul's statement here it's mission statement. A fragmented Church re-united in faith in anticipation and preparation of Jesus' return as The Righteous Judge and living in The Promise of that accounting. Perfected in that faith defined in Hebrews 11.

The connection between obedience and Jesus' death on the Cross is brought out in Hebrews 5:8-10 NIV. *"During the days of Jesus' life on earth, he offered up prayers and petitions with loud cries and tears to the one who could save him from death, and he was heard because of his reverent submission. Although he was a son, he learned obedience from what he suffered and once made perfect, he became the source of eternal salvation for all who obey him and was designated to be high priest in the order of Melchiedek."* This seems to bring out Jesus' faith and trust in His Father to save Him from death and sets the example for us. Jesus is saved from death by faith in His Father. He is perfected in this faith, trust and obedience, and when he comes back, He becomes the source of eternal salvation for all those who trust and obey Him perfected in that faith and promised reward.

The Pure Word Translation brings a clearer view of what the writer is trying to get across here in verses 8 and 9, *"Even though He is a Son, He Learned Obedience from the things suffered by His Choice. And Being Made Perfect, He Became the Author of Eternal Salvation to All That Obey Him."* The benefit of Jesus' work on the cross is limited to those who trust and obey him. Jesus was born the perfect sacrifice and, as our High Priest, was uniquely qualified to die for the sins of the world. This is the pattern of our learning as we choose to trust in God also and obey His Commands.

I hear so often in songs and sermons that "He took my place, He bore my cross" and "salvation full and free" that this lie must be being taught in evangelical seminaries everywhere. I am not qualified to die for the sins of the world and He bore my sin not my cross - He took my shame; He took my guilt. This passage in Hebrews, limits atonement to the obedient and flies in the face of Post Modern Theology that is being taught in seminaries today and the Limited Atonement of Calvinism based on belief.

Limited Atonement is perhaps the most important pillar of the theology of predestination - from the beginning of time God has chosen those who will receive the gift of atonement and eternal life. Jesus' warning to His disciples after He teaches them to pray gives us a true picture of limited atonement as He tells them, *"but if you do not forgive men their sins, your father will not forgive your sins."*, Matthew 6:15. Thus He limits the benefit of His death on the Cross to those who obey His instructions.

It becomes clear in Luke 9;18-27 that Limited Atonement is something that happens by our choice as we choose to follow Jesus. It is not something that God chooses for us from the beginning of time. This passage in Luke begins with Peter's confession and has the elements of God's plan of salvation concluding with, *"If anyone is ashamed of me and my words (teaching), the son of man will be ashamed of him when he comes in his glory and in the glory of the Father and of the holy angels. I tell you the truth, some who are standing here will not taste death before they see the kingdom of God."*, verses 26 and 27. Please read this for yourself and see how verses 23 and 24 are used to show who is saved and who is not.

The saved mind-set exists in the church culture today because of this misunderstanding of Limited Atonement. No one is saved without a lifelong, single minded commitment to trust and obey God's commands and Jesus' instructions. Salvation can only happen when Jesus comes back in His Glory for a final accounting and the awarding of eternal life "on that Day". Having an eternally saved status in this life is a myth. The obedient go from living in The Promise – to living in The Land of The Promise instantly when Jesus returns.

Followers are chosen for a mission, not a destination, and are to obey that calling as a matter of faith. It is a faith that is so simple that a child can understand it. If our children grew up in that faith, it would become second nature to them as their parents teach them obedience. *"And he said, "I tell you the truth, unless you change and become like little children, you will never enter the kingdom of heaven.",* Matthew 18:3.

Reading around this, it is apparent that teaching a child to believe in Jesus is job #1. But then to teach them, the rest of their lives, that belief is what gets them to heaven instantly, would be wrong and could be seen by them as a means to escape this sin sick world leaving all of their sorrows behind. Instant heaven has become an escape hatch for many, of all ages, to escape their pain and misery in this world and then to arrive at a promised Paradise. As obedient children of God doing our assigned work, our destination is an accounting before entering The Kingdom. This is the same faith that Jesus instilled in those First-Century followers – Faith in The Promise One and His promise to return as The Righteous Judge for this accounting.

We are in the age of grace between Jesus's return to heaven and His coming again out of heaven. We are given a Gospel of Love; it is the Gospel of hope; it is the Gospel of joyful obedience; it is the Gospel that holds the Church together; and it is the Gospel that puts his children to work, sharing that Gospel, on the narrow road that leads to life eternal.

Chapter #7
Dullness of Mind

The 400 years of darkness between Malachi and Matthew maybe repeating itself in today's culture. Has the age of grace become the age of darkness due to having a saved mindset? For the Jewish leadership, The Promised One had become a warrior king to rid themselves of the Romans and clean up that mess. Their inability to comprehend a savior of a different sort brought them to the point of killing the very one who would fulfill The Promise. If the leaders of today's Christian Culture hold on to the appearance of Jesus as the suffering servant and do not move on to Him as Righteous Judge, they will be guilty of the same transgression and creating a bigger mess.

Hebrews chapters 5–10 is a sobering warning of falling away from faith in the coming of the Righteous Judge. Let's focus on one paragraph, Hebrews 6:4 to 6-6: *"It is impossible for those who have once been enlightened, who have tasted the heavenly gift, who have shared in the Holy Spirit, who have tasted the goodness of the word of God and the powers of the coming age, if they fall away, to be brought back to repentance, because to their loss they are crucifying the Son of God all over again and subjecting him to public disgrace."*

The writer is talking to the culture of his time and, of course, our time and culture also. Making this one long sentence makes it hard to understand and even harder to digest. It seems obvious this is pointing out that getting our faith wrong (weak) defeats Jesus' work on the cross. This is why I say that a genuine saving faith is in The Promise more than the person. That same saved mind-set of those Jewish leaders puts today's culture in the same darkness that the Jewish culture was in 2000 years ago and we are crucifying the Righteous Judge even before he comes.

The Jewish leaders had designed a messiah that suited them better than the one God sent them. A warrior king is what they wanted and in their resistance to adjust to God's design, they helped create the image of the suffering servant. They refused to be changed by the true Messiah and held on to the designer Jesus they had created that suited them better. This same dynamic is at work in the minds of Christian leaders today. Our culture would rather hold on to the image of the suffering servant than to put our faith in the coming Righteous Judge. We don't want the image we have of Jesus to change because that would require us to change. Jesus has been the Righteous Judge from the beginning of time and will be to the end of time.

"Seek ye first the kingdom of God and his righteousness", comes from the mouth of the Righteous Judge. Wanting to live in His Kingdom forever is the motivation to seek His righteousness and allows God to change us. This is why it is so important to put our faith in the "Soon Coming King" rather than the image of Jesus in His first appearing. We can create a messiah that suits us and a faith in an image of God that requires little if any change in us.

Paul's new faith demanded that he become a new creature and his saved mind-set was the first thing that had to go. Jesus was not going to be just a nice addition to what he already believed. Paul's focus on The Second Coming is the best evidence that God was changing him into a man that suited Him.

Evangelism is a rare commodity in today's culture because the saved mind-set demands nothing from us and everything from Jesus. How much different is this attitude in the church from the attitude in our culture outside The Church. Just give me your money (taxes or tithes) and live productive lives (optional) for the country or the kingdom. These are two parallel universes, looking at one, you can see the other. It is so important to see faith in The Promise One - the coming Jesus - who fulfills The Promise as He brings salvation with Him at His return.

CHAPTER #8
Storge Love

God's justice demands that everyone have an equal opportunity for salvation. He is not willing that anyone should perish. His justice also demands obedience from all those who will enter His Kingdom. Obedience is a lifestyle of genuine faith, righteous acts of service that build up The Kingdom and a life lived in The Promise of Salvation. God's gift of Grace is in that promise as Kingdom workers offer that same promise to the world around them.

God's Agape Love is freely given to all of His creatures. Jesus invites all to believe and become members of God's Family set apart for The Kingdom. Once a person is in the family, Family Love – Storge Love demands that all in the family learn, preach and teach obedience to God's Commands. This shields God's Family from Satan's attack as they wage war on the enemy and his offer of instant gratification salvation. Speaking truth in love, tough love, is the glue that will hold The Family of God together – unified in this Storge Love from generation to generation.

The Kairos Prison Ministry, in which I take part, uses the principals of Storge Love to a great extent. We have table groups that become like families. These accountability groups are to continue after our four day sessions end. We also encourage team members to form similar accountability groups on the outside. We impress upon them that lone wolf faith invites Satan's attack, that apart from the family, the church, nothing will change and that their accountability group will help keep them on the narrow road with each step they take on their journey.

A personal note: The last time we did our four-day retreat; I gave a talk on '"Friendship with God". In the preview, I was told that I used the word obedience too much. This tells me that my message was, to those men, total obedience equals total victory. And then I come home to a church that expects complete victory with partial or even no obedience - don't even mention the word. Telling those new Christians that obedience was the thing that would keep them safe from Satan's attack on their journey to judgment was the most important thing I said to them. I hope and pray they hold on to that belief as long as they live.

Paul's letter to the Ephesians is a great example of this Storge Love. It comes with instructions on how The Family of God should operate and to promote and encourage non-believers to become part of that family. One of the most important qualities of Storge Love is tough love. God's plan of salvation begins and ends with tough love. For example, God's affectionate love for Adam and Eve is evident in The Creation Story. God's righteousness demands that He banish them from Paradise because of their disobedience. And then when Jesus comes back as The Righteous Judge, He will lift that curse and welcome, into Paradise, those who have been obedient, living a lifestyle worthy of their calling. The bite of the apple brought death because of their disobedience and that has not changed. Disobedient lifestyles, whatever they may be, will bring about that same punishment in the last day. God has not changed and the punishment has not changed either.

Those who continue living in disobedience, believing that lifestyle doesn't matter, will be banished forever at Judgment, and eternally separated from The Family of God. The Creation Story is the best example of the connection between obedience and living in the presence of God: then; now; and forever more. All of God's Commands and Jesus' instructions come into play and are there to guide us on our journey. They are not there to punish us, they are there to keep us safe on our journey and safe from God's wrath and anger when Jesus comes back.

Paul writes about this consequence in Romans Chapter 2, verses 6-8. *"But because of your stubbornness and unrepentant heart, you are storing up wrath against yourself for the day of God's wrath when his righteous judgment will be revealed. God will give to each person according to what he has done. To those who by persistence in doing good seek glory, honor and immortality, he will give eternal life. But for those who are self-seeking and who reject the truth and follow evil, there will be wrath and anger."* This is the good news - bad news story of the Gospel according to Paul. Then there is this from 1 Thessalonians Chapter 1:10, *"and to wait for his son from heaven, who he raised from the dead - Jesus, who rescues us from the coming wrath."*

Jesus makes this happen for us at the end of Matthew in Chapter 28 when He says this, *"Therefore go and make disciples of all nations, baptizing them in the name of the Father and of the Son of the Holy Spirit, and teaching them to obey everything I have commanded you. And surely I am with you always, to the very end of the age."* This passage is a Catch 22 statement – those who live disobedient lifestyles cannot teach obedience and those who choose not to teach obedience, for whatever reason, are being disobedient. Everyone in the family of God should be in some stage of both learning and teaching obedience.

This Great Commission is the very thing that rescues us from God's wrath. This instruction completes Jesus' mission to rescue, to save the whole world according to The Gospel of Matthew. His followers must continue to teach, preach and learn obedience in order to rescue that same world from God's wrath before The Second Coming. The age of Grace, The Church Age, then becomes a race against time to bring as many into The Family of God as that time allows.

Jesus comes to lift the curse that God subjected His creation to, at the beginning. At The Second Coming, those who have done good, living a holy - obedient lifestyle, will be protected from God's wrath and judged worthy of life in Paradise. Paul writes about this race, fight and reward in 2Timothy 4:6-8 which I quoted, in part, earlier. Paul also writes about living under the curse and the lifting of the curse in Romans Chapter 8:18-25. *"For the creation was subjected to frustration, not by its own choice, but by the will of the one who subjected it, in hope that the creation itself will be liberated from its bondage to decay and brought into the glorious freedom of the children of God."*, verses 20 and 21.

CHAPTER #9
The Family of God

The knowledge gleaned from Ephesians chapters 4-6 and Hebrews Chapters 4-6 bring to mind again Matthew 18:3, *"And he said, 'I tell you the truth, unless you change and become like little children. you will never enter the kingdom of heaven."* Do not enter The Family of God as an adult thinking you know it all with your carnal, disobedient mind. God's Agape love brings one into the family like a welcome mat at the front door. But they need the mother's milk of Storge Love to grow up as an unrepentant heart grows into a repentant heart.

A rewiring of the mind must take place as the mind of Christ is planted into that babe. It's not that we continue in a childlike faith, it's that one must mature into an obedient adult, worthy of and able to teach others to be obedient and, "...grow in the grace and knowledge of our Lord and Savior Jesus Christ.", even if only by example. Chances are that a disobedient child will grow up into a disobedient adult and damage the family in any circumstance. This is why it is so clear that teaching obedience must be done at every stage of life. And as obedient children of God we will be witnesses to His Glory and The Promise.

This Storge love is an affectionate love that protects the family from within and from without. Jesus' obedience to the will of His father, on the cross, sets the standard for the Christian Lifestyle. The question begs to ask, why do any of this if you are already saved or more exactly, if you are saved at the moment of belief? Agape love is what God's children take into the world – Storge love keeps them safe as they go.

The antonym of Storge Love is Astorge which can be defined as heartless - an uncaring, indifferent attitude. Paul uses Astorge to describe those who believe in God but willfully do not obey His commands. The word, Astorge appears near the end of Romans Chapter 1 and near the beginning of 2 Timothy Chapter 3. *"Although they know God's righteous decree that those who do such things deserve death, they not only continue to do these very things but also approve of those who practice them."*, Romans 1:32. *"They are the kind who worm (creep) their way into homes (bedrooms) and gain control over weak-willed (foolish) Woman..."*, 2Timothy 3:6. By using Astorge to describe a willful disobedient lifestyle, it's antonym Storge, not found in Scripture, would then become a word that describes, by default, a - loving - affectionate attitude and an obedient lifestyle.

Paul's passion on identifying this disobedient lifestyle is evident in that he describes his history of being part of that lifestyle. *"At one time we too were foolish, disobedient, deceived and enslaved by all kinds of passions and pleasure. We lived in malice and envy, being hated and hating one another."*, Titus 3:3. This statement begins his description of his own conversion. It is a beautiful passage of a renewed faith and being born anew, living in hope of eternal life. And just for good measure, *"For it is not those hear the law who are righteous in God's sight, but it is those who obey the law who will be declared righteous."*, Romans 2:13.

In these two passages from Romans and 2 Timothy above, Paul is describing a willful disobedient lifestyle practiced by many in The Church today. What one generation tolerates, the next generation embraces. The obedient lifestyle is key to entering The Kingdom. Marketing hope in Jesus' return and that promised reward is key to the survival of The Family of

God. Not locked in a prison of entitlement that Paul describes in Titus above.

"Therefore, since the promise of entering his rest still stands, let us be careful that none of you be found to have fallen short of it. For we also have had the gospel preached to us, just as they did, but the message they heard was of no value to them, because those who heard did not combine it with faith." The first three verses of Hebrews 4. Also, *"Nothing in all creation is hidden from God's sight. Everything is uncovered and laid bare before the eyes of him to whom we must give an account.",* verse 14.

In its introduction to Ephesians, The NIV Bible says this in part, *"One of Paul's themes in Ephesians is that of unity and God's purpose 'to bring all things in heaven and on earth together under one head, even Christ.' Because of this unity, Paul wrote, all Christians are one family in Jesus, and they should act with love toward each other. He gives believers instructions on how to "live a life of love" by addressing the husband-wife, parent-child, and slave-master relationships".* Storge love - Ephesians - a message in a bottle for today's Family of God.

Here and throughout Scripture we have these instructions of Storge love: Children, obey your parents; Husbands love your wives; Slaves, obey your masters. And the inverse: Parents, love your children; Wives, love your husbands; masters, love your slaves/servants. This describes a top-down, bottom-up lifestyle that is under assault today. The socialist transformation of America begins with hatred and the destruction of the family and ends with the destruction of The Church – The Family of God.

It has been pointed out to me that the word Storge doesn't appear in the new testament. What a shame or better yet, maybe God didn't see the need since He put it in our DNA. Family love is in our DNA: a mother's love for her child even before it is born; a father's love for his child even before it is born and of course love between all those in the family especially when brought up in the special affectionate love of God through Jesus Christ and God's desire for that family to live eternally with Him in His Paradise.

The idea of a tender-hearted God seems to have been suppressed in the early Church. Sinful man on the hands of a righteous God was prevalent and is evident in the King James Bible. There are at least three events in Jesus' life that reveal this tender-hearted God. Jesus met a lifelong friend as they hung on their crosses. One of those two thieves, being crucified with him, must have realized who Jesus was, maybe revealed to him by The Holy Spirit, when he said to Jesus, "Remember me when you come into your kingdom." Jesus made him the promise of the ages when he says, "you will be with me in paradise." The thief believed who Jesus was and put his faith and trust in that promise. What else could he do? Jesus gave him a hope and a promise that this is not all there is, there is a Paradise that awaits His friends – including this new one.

Not long before this, Jesus came to tears as he came to the aid of three friends. Jesus had befriended a family of two sisters and their brother Lazarus in the village of Bethany. The two sisters, Mary and Martha, sent word to Jesus that Lazarus was sick. Jesus did not respond immediately, but waited, knowing that Lazarus was at the point of dying. Lazarus had been in the tomb four days when He did arrive. Martha heard He was coming and went to meet Him, "Lord," Martha said to Jesus, "if you had been here, my brother would not have died." Jesus said to her, "Your brother will rise again." Martha answered, "I know he will rise again at the last day." As this event unfolds in John Chapter eleven, it reveals Jesus' tender heart and also what Jesus had taught Martha about The Resurrection.

And then, we have Jesus' encounter with Peter close to the end of John's Gospel Chapter 21:15-17. From The Pure Word, *"Then, when they had dined, Jesus said to Simon Peter son of Jonas, are you Loving (agapoa, pure unselfish love) Me greater than these?*

He said to Him Emphatically, Yes, Oh Lord, You Spiritually know that I affectionately love (phileo, brotherly love) You. He Said to him, You must Feed My Lambs. He Said to him, again, the second time, Oh Simon Jonas, are you Loving (agapoa) Me? He Said to him, Emphatically Yes, Oh Lord. You Spiritually Know that I affectionately love (phileo) You? He Said to him, You must Shepherd My Sheep. He Said to him a third time, Oh Simon Peter, do you affectionately love (phileo) Me? Peter was made grieved, because He Spoke to him a third time. Are you affectionately loving (phileo) Me? So then he spoke to Him, Oh Lord, you Spiritually Know all things, You Know that I affectionately love (phileo) You. Jesus Said to him, Feed My Sheep."

The major elements of family love including: mother's milk; care and protection; and spiritually feeding all in the family; are here without using the phrase Storge Love. This phrase for tender-hearted affection needs to be part of our understanding of God's love and understood along with other phrases like tough love and speaking truth in love. This needs to be at the heart of how we teach obedience to people of all ages which leads to being ready and watching for The Second Coming. The Old Testament meaning of grace, God's tender loving care (TLC), needs to be brought into the New Testament and stop conflating the word grace with salvation.

Peter is faithful to fulfill this challenge as he writes his letters. Reading the first chapter of his second letter, we find a complete instruction for The Family of God beginning with faith in His promise to return. In part he writes this about family values, add to your faith: goodness; then knowledge; then self-control; then perseverance; then godliness; and then, brotherly kindness (phileo); and then love (agape). Here, you have the keys to The Kingdom, not in Peter's hands, but in his letters.

I have made this point in my last book and it bears repeating here in the context of Storge Love – Family Love. This does not happen instantly. But it must happen in The Family of God to make sure of a rich welcome into the Eternal Kingdom as you teach these things in preparation for The Second Coming. *"We did not follow cleverly invented stories when we told you about the power and coming of our Lord Jesus Christ...",* verse 1:16.

Today's fragmented church has failed to follow Paul's instruction in Ephesians 4:11-13. A fragmented church must compete with each other for supporters. The mission then becomes - how to attract more people to your church and the element of obedience dies on the vine along with a unified faith. People, spoiled by free grace and easy belief, would seldom if ever be attracted to a recovery program unless they have hit rock bottom in their journey. A destructive lifestyle is usually the factor that moves people to hit rock bottom and the hopelessness that can hit people at any time and for many reasons.

There would seem to be two main routes of escaping this reality - a recovery program of tough love to escape that destructive lifestyle or just complete the road to destruction, lay down and die. Die in the false hope of instant heaven. The Paradise that Jesus promised to that thief on the cross was not instant heaven. Again, it must be remembered what the thief said to Jesus at that moment, "Remember me when you come into your kingdom." That moment is yet to come, but "on that Day" of resurrection, all of God's creatures will rise out of the dust of the earth to face The Righteous Judge. A moment of accountability – Storge Love – tough love, and God's Righteousness as He sorts the Sheep from the Goats.

When I look at all that I have written in this chapter, a very simple and easily understood Plan of Salvation comes into view that even a child can understand. Man's disobedience gets him excluded from paradise – man's obedience will get him included and returned to paradise. It's just that simple.

CHAPTER #10
The Calvinized Christian Culture

Digging deeply in to God's word has been very rewarding and has given me something new to share with the whole world. The problem is that I come in conflict with what I believe is a very shallow reading of Scripture. I, like John Wesley, believe that the fundamentals of Calvinism are evil and require a flawed reading of Scripture. The idea that God has predestined some people to be excluded from the kingdom paints a picture of a heartless god. God's righteousness and justice requires that all of His creatures have the same opportunity to become His children and part of His Family.

It is hard for me to not to feel chosen by God to be a writer and bring a different way of understanding to Scripture. But at the beginning of that journey, I had the freedom to say no. I know now that to say no would have been the most stupid and wrong decision of my life. I like the word preordained and the purpose of a journey and mission that ends in a meeting with the one who preordained that journey. "It's about the journey, not the destination." A quote by Harley Davidson.

Most of the words we find in Scripture that describe a disobedient lifestyle are hedonistic in nature. We have a very long list of these words and lifestyles in the first chapter of Romans and elsewhere. In the theology of the early Calvinists, man had no righteousness of his own, all righteousness came from God. God's righteousness had to be imputed into man because man had none of his own. Out of this came the belief that man would or could continue to sin. And out of this hedonistic approach to faith came John Wesley who said no, not so, and then came the holiness movement that was associated with him.

Looking at the history of the Calvinist movement, I see a theology that allowed a hedonistic, sexually promiscuous culture of that time, to have the hope of heaven in spite of their sinful lifestyles. No need to go further here accept to say that there is a lot of this and more going on in today's church. It is part of Post Modern Theology that lifestyle doesn't matter. In the past, most of this went on behind closed doors. Today, a lot of this bad behavior goes on out in the open and it all has its roots in Calvinism. It is said about those who die in this lifestyle, "From the arms of a harlot, to the arms of God".

Recently, by sheer coincidence, I met a Wesleyan pastor, Daniel E. LeRoy. He had written two books similar to mine - his writing coming against the domination of Calvinist Doctrine in The Wesleyan Church. In his book, "Rediscovering Our Holiness Heritage" there is a chapter titled, " The Baptistification of the Wesleyan Church". It captures, in a nutshell, the focus of my latest book "on that Day'. In a much kinder and gentler way he identifies much of the problem that I identify, to include Post Modern Theology. My experience causes me to feel like, no matter where I go to church, I am a Wesleyan in a Baptist Church.

After I had published my first book, I knew that it was poorly written but had some very good insights. At that time, I prayed that someone, who was a better writer, would like my ideas and do a better job of writing and putting them in a book. Meeting Dan, I feel now like God answered my prayer. Dan was writing that book about the same time that I was writing mine. Dan, writing with the gentleness of a pastor and me, coming against the whole Christian Culture, like a bull in a china shop.

I have touched on hopelessness and feel the need to expand on that human condition. Polls are showing that hopelessness is on the rise and replacing the American Dream in our country. There are those in our national government who want to fundamentally transform us into a socialist society. Where ever socialism is tried, it is always accompanied by hopelessness and millions of premature deaths.

With a government that promotes the hope of a socialist utopia and with a church that promotes instant heaven at the moment of death - we have a perfect storm in this country. Both cultures are being locked in a prison of entitlement. Satan is using both of these lies to destroy our way of life which is on the march across the globe. Freedom and obedience to our Constitution are under assault which is coming from many directions. Leaders in The Church are promoting rebellion and disobedience to God's Commandments. Leaders in our government are promoting rebellion and disobedience to the laws of our nation and our way of life. It all comes down to lifestyle.

In my opinion, there are two college professors who are leading the charge in this WOKE agenda - the fundamental transformation of our nation into a socialist society. One, a convicted insurrectionist who got out of prison on a technicality, and the other one, who promised that we were five days away from the fundamental transformation of America. They are both, behind the scene, directing that agenda in our government and in our universities. Note: A family member told me recently what WOKE stands for, "Willfully Overlooking Known Evil" - works for me.

In this perfect storm, Post Modern Theology has firmly taken control of our seminaries and until that stops we have little hope. The American Dream and the dream of Paradise at Jesus' Second Coming will die together in a global war. Jesus is not coming back to clean up this mess like the Jews wanting a warrior king to clean up their mess. He is coming back to gather those who, through obedience, have overcome this world so as to enter the next world.

What I see happening in America today and over the last two and a half centuries is a microcosm of what has happened in The Church over the last twenty centuries. This country was founded by men who loved God, but is now run by evil men who love power and money. One is mostly run by unelected officials in a too powerful bureaucracy. The other is run mostly by unelected professors who love the power of their secure positions and the money that comes with that. They live in a spiritually bankrupt world of higher learning, training our next generation of church leaders and government officials leading to a world without hope or maybe a false hope.

When I get into discussions with these moderniacs, I experience what I call the Baptist beat down. They seem to be trained in spiritual warfare in fighting with anyone who would challenge their heartless theology. And when they preach, they sometimes raise their voice to browbeat this theology down our throats or into our brains.

The heartless god of Post Modern Theology has a lot in common with the heartless god of socialism, Big Brother. They both make promises that are not true. In The Creation Story, the serpent offers instant self-gratification and in Jesus' encounter with Satan, he also offers instant self-gratification along with "worship me". Big Brother is the god of big government and offers free everything. "From each according to their ability - to each according to their need." "Salvation - Full and Free" is the slogan of the post-modern theologians. Both seem to have the same god in common - a god of instant self-gratification.

Post Modern Theology has its roots in historic Calvinism and a saved mind-set. Not having that saved mind-set is taboo and makes one, who disagrees, a dangerous outsider - a trouble maker. The Armenian belief that Calvin was wrong is unacceptable and is not tolerated in today's Christian Culture.

Just like in a socialist society, rebellion against that socialist commune will not be tolerated either.

John Wesley rebelled against the theology of Calvin in a way that caught on in England, but not in America, because George Whitfield came to America to found a Methodist Church rooted in Calvinism. The Armenian belief associated with John Wesley is seldom if ever part of organized religion in America because the vast majority here, have that saved mind-set and hold on to that belief. To disagree with that, in evangelical circles, is something that is not tolerated. I know because I have experienced that, and others I have met, feel the same way. So, what to do now? Start a new Holy Club where the Calvinist dogma of predestination is not tolerated and maybe another Great Awakening will happen looking forward to His appearing and the redemption Jesus brings with Him.

CHAPTER #11
The I Never Knew You Crowd

Obedience is the means by which we are redeemed. Down through the centuries, man has devised many formulas for man's redemption. None that I have heard require obedience – only faith and belief. I touched on this problem earlier but God seems to want me to dig deeper on the idea. Paul wrestles with the idea that the things he ought to do he resists and the things he ought not to do he does not resist. Paul's formula very much connects obedience with salvation.

This is a matter of will. *"Not everyone who says to me, 'Lord, Lord,' will enter the kingdom of heaven, but only he who does the will of my Father who is in heaven...",* Matthew 7:21. Our will must be replaced with God's will. In this passage, the instruction of doing God's will be absolute. God's will is that we obey His Commands. Jesus says this, "If you love me, you will obey me." There is a great resistance to obedience in the hearts of men. When you tell a child not to do something, they seem to respond by doing exactly what they were told not to do at their first opportunity. For me, this is a big can of worms and avoiding the issue of obedience in any salvation message is a grave mistake.

When I speak to friends about this reality, I am met with total resistance. Instead, I hear about man's total depravity or man's total inability to do anything good without a divine encounter. It would follow that without this encounter, man is totally incapable of obedience to the will of God. In Matthew chapter 7, Jesus follows verse 21 with this, *"Many will say to me on that day, 'Lord, Lord, did we not prophecy in your name, and in your name drive out demons and perform many miracles?' Then I will tell them plainly, 'I never knew you. Away from me, you evil doers!'* " These believers become the "I never knew you" church. They talk about their many miracles, have their good works and great preachers, but their saved mind-set, instant heaven and disobedient lifestyles are apart from the will of God.

Like many others, this passage flies in the face of this idea that man is totally incapable doing the will of the Father by his own choice. Following this passage, we find The Wise and Foolish Builders. *"Therefore, everyone who hears these words of mine and puts them into practice is like a wise man who built his house on the rock. The rain came down, the streams rose, and the winds blew and beat against that house; yet it did not fall, because it had its foundation on the rock."*, verses 24 and 25. Choosing to put into practice Jesus' instructions is the point here and doing the will of the Father is by man's own choice. To believe that man is totally incapable of making a right decision here, is to say that Jesus condemns those evil doers by withholding His righteousness from them.

There is a larger issue here that no one seems to see. These evil doers have done all the right things trusting in their own goodness. They call Jesus Lord, and in His name prophesy and drive out demons and perform many miracles; all with which they are pleased and has been done out in the open. The evil that they have done must be hidden from view - behind closed doors. Jesus sees what they are doing behind those closed doors, their willful disobedient behavior and evil lifestyles. They will be cast out on our Day of Judgment just like Adam and Eve were cast out of Paradise for their willful disobedience on their Day of Judgment.

We can pass on to our children, by teaching and by example, a faith that ignores the reality of Final Judgment or a faith that prepares them for that event and The Coming Wrath. In either case, God's love and how we experience that love is at stake and how youthful minds handle those two very different views. We can instill in them a sense of entitlement to a heavenly reward at their death or, much better, a devoted affection that is shared in The Family of God as they journey to that promised Day of reward. Not locked in a prison of entitlement, but looking forward to a promotion, or maybe a diploma, or maybe just a pure gift for having lived a life pleasing to God and the joy of a celebration at Jesus' return.

The dreadful things that Jesus describes in Matthew 7, happen "on that Day", the Day of God's Wrath - the Day of Judgment. Who are the "I never knew you" crowd in today's church? Jesus describes two very different lifestyles here: one of wise obedience to His instructions; and one of foolish disobedience to His instructions. This then becomes the deciding factor on who survives these calamities. The obedient lifestyle then becomes the foundation of what saves us. Living in The Promise is the most important thing that we do to help Jesus choose who gets into His Paradise.

Here, Jesus makes lifestyle the main thing that brings salvation, but of course it is not the only thing. Not forgetting that God's goodness, mercy and compassion rests on those He chooses, (Ref. Exodus 33:19). It follows that those in today's church that teach and preach that our lifestyles don't matter are the "I never knew you" crowd - doing all the right things while believing, preaching and teaching the wrong thing to everyone all the while promoting the "I never knew you" church.

CHAPTER #12
The Jesus that I Know

The formula for salvation found in Scripture starts with John the Baptist. "But when he saw many of the Pharisees and Sadducees coming to where he was baptizing, he said to them, *"You brood of vipers! Who warned you to flee the coming wrath? Produce fruit in keeping with repentance."*, Matthew Chapter 3:7-8. This was right before Jesus began preaching, "Repent for the kingdom of heaven is near." It is obvious that in a church where lifestyle doesn't matter, people will want God to bless their disobedient lifestyles because they have no righteousness of their own and are therefore unrepentant in their continued disobedience.

The *"...Jesus, who rescues us from the coming wrath."*, 1 Thess. 1:10, explains His point here in Matthew Chapter 13. In the Parable of the Sower, Jesus tell us what the problem is, *"But while everyone was sleeping, the enemy came and sowed weeds among the wheat, and went away."*, verse 25. Then later, in the Parable of the Weeds Explained, Jesus says this about the end of the age, *"The Son of Man will send out his angels, and they will weed out of his kingdom everything that causes sin and all who do evil. They will throw them into the fiery furnace, where there will be weeping and gnashing of teeth"*, verses 41 and 42.

The idea that at the moment of belief one is saved, eternally secure and destined for heaven is associated with John Calvin. He was a Sixteenth- Century French-Catholic Lawyer. The culture in France has, for centuries, been Hedonistic. Sexual promiscuity was part of that culture then and has been associated with that culture up to today. His theology has come down to us through evangelical seminaries without much change.

John Wesley was exposed to this hedonism, probably for the first time, when he went off to seminary. His Holiness Doctrine probably had a lot to do with his response to what he experienced at Oxford. His mother Susanna may have been the first woman holiness preacher as she raised her children. Her sons, John and Charles, continued in this holiness lifestyle and a tradition was born. John said this about Oxford, "It would be better for those students if they would be trained to be Christian before they were trained to be priests". Hedonism in The Church had crossed the English Channel and did not stop there.

One of the pillars of the Calvinist movement is that the disobedient lifestyles of that time could continue and a believer would still be saved. The faith that resulted from this theology avoided (fled) God's Wrath and Righteous Judgment at The Second Coming. This appeals to man's instant self-gratification nature and especially in one's own sexuality. John Wesley rebelled against this theology and its apparent rebellion against holy living and The Second Coming. How convenient it is for church leaders to preach instant salvation and instant heaven to all and avoid (flee) the reality of God's Wrath being poured out on the disobedient at Judgment.

Those who believe and teach this dogma will have a rude awakening when they are called out of the grave as The Trumpet sounds at Jesus Christ's Second Coming. It looks to me like John Calvin dreamed up a way for Christians to live a disobedient, hedonistic lifestyle and still be welcomed into heaven when they died. Down through the centuries, this theology has been refined, improved and promoted to the joyous relief of those who want to live like hell and have salvation also.

There is a wave of disobedient/unrepentant lifestyles taking over the Christian Church today. This says to the world that lifestyle doesn't matter in today's church or anywhere else, for that matter. Trying to get around this issue has gone on for centuries. The Catholic Church selling indulgences to build the Sistine Chapel was mainly about buying unrepentant loved one's way into heaven. Today, we have Gay Revisionist Theology competing for our young people with their designer Jesus. Passing this broad road approach to salvation on to our children assures destruction for the next generation and all who believe, teach and preach, and practice disobedient lifestyles.

Martin Luther's reformation rebelled against the idea of selling indulgences. About the same time, John Calvin led a movement saying that confession plus repentance made disobedience okay because we had no righteousness of our own. The disobedient lifestyle would or could continue. Thus a morally impure spirit has gradually replaced The Holy Spirit in Christ's Church. This new spirit has, for the most part, made holiness a non-issue. Two hundred years later John Wesley came along and rebelled against Calvin's theology by saying that a holy lifestyle and a life lived free from the desire to sin was the main thing. But today, man's desire to make lifestyle and Final Judgment a non-issue may finally be winning over the Christian Culture.

Calvinism ignores the fact that we have been freely gifted with The Holy Spirit and yet in their theology, only those who have been chosen by God receive that gift and are saved at the moment of belief. This suggests that the spirit of Calvinism is very selective of who receives that spirit and assumes that no one has received The Holy Spirit prior to that divine appointment. This then becomes their ticket to heaven as salvation is freely given to all of those who believe in this dogma. The free gift of The Holy Spirit has been replaced with the free gift of grace, salvation is thus assured by receiving this morally impure spirit into the heart. Without any change in behavior, the label of Christian is applied to the new believer and the instant gratification crowd has brought another soul into Satan's camp.

Not only does the instant gratification crowd corrupt the image of Jesus, they also have corrupted the image of The Holy Spirit. The main purpose of The Holy Spirit is to purify The Family of God on their journey to Judgment. John Wesley defined this as sanctification on the journey to perfection. *"And do not grieve the holy spirit of God, with whom you were sealed for the day of redemption."*, Ephesians 4:30. This should also grieve all those who are being purified by The Holy Spirit on their way to the Day of Redemption.

Daniel's Prophesy is coming true, *"But when you Spiritually Discern the abomination of desolation, that Spirit Spoken by Daniel the Profit, standing whereto he ought defiantly not. He that reads must be comprehending, then those inside Judaea must flee to the mountains."*, Mark 13:14, The Pure Word. This is referring to the abomination of desolation found in Daniel 11:31 and 12:11. A church led by a morally impure spirit cannot or will not comprehend this prophecy and will be caught unaware at The Second Coming. God is storing up His Wrath for this future moment in time, for those whose repentance is insincere and momentary at their conversion and arrive at Judgment clueless, full of regret - weeping and gnashing their teeth.

In the first forty-eight verses of Romans, Paul preaches his Gospel and describes for us this abomination of desolation that we find in Mark 13:14. The problem is that obedience is a lifetime lifestyle that must be taught from day one in The Family of God. Regardless of when someone is born into The Family of God, true repentance with true faith in The Promise must be taught to glorify God who first made that promise to Father Abraham.

This is The Gospel according to Paul as he writes in Romans, *"This will take place on the day when God will judge men's secrets through Jesus Christ, as my gospel declares."*, the 48th verse. The

Gospel of Paul is the Gospel of Jesus Christ - a Journey to Judgment - from disobedience to obedience and The Second Coming, "Your kingdom come Your will be done on earth as it is in heaven.".

This is a battle inside The Family of God and is between those filled with The Holy Spirit and those filled with a morally impure spirit. This is a battle that must be fought - lifestyles that please or displease our God. The fate of The Church lies in the balance. This is much the same battle that is going on in our country today where lifestyle and morality are at stake and the survival of our country, as it was founded, is also at stake.

Donald Trump clearly sees himself as the one to lead in the battle to save us from those who hate our country as it was founded. The Obama nation that many desire leading to the decimation of our economy (Bidenomics) will lead to one world order and the demise of The Church. For a while there will be a new replacement church that will replace The (true) Family of God. All of this playing on man's desire to create his own utopian existence as a means to return to Paradise. Socialism is a lie and not the solution to man's desire to return to paradise - obedience to God's Commands is the solution and returns man to paradise.

God is storing up His Wrath against those who are the problem and also those who isolate themselves from the problem. Remember Jesus said, "upon this rock, I will build my church and the gates of hell will not prevail against it." Jesus said this at Caesaria Philippi which was at the center of Satan's camp and the worship of the god pan. Jesus knows that He is building His Church right in the middle of Satan's camp. Jesus cannot be savior of the world when His Church runs away from the problem or becomes part of the problem. At the heart of these replacement churches will be a designer Jesus, custom made for their faith and blessing their lifestyles. Better a little tough love now than a whole lot at Christ's return.

CHAPTER #13
The Collaboration Leading to the Destination

Many friends have influenced me and what I have written, but two stand out above the many. The Reverend Bob Baldwin is the friend who challenged me to write a book and at the very first helped me see that I was taking on the whole Christian Culture. And then there is I. J. (Jerry) Payne, a friend from long before I started writing. I stayed in close contact with these two friends as I wrote, one with a pastor's perspective and the other with a layman's perspective.

Before I began to write books, Jerry and I became involved in business. I owned the business and Jerry managed the business. Jerry had a degree in electrical engineering with a minor in English. For me wanting to write, this was a match made in heaven. We were in daily contact and, as I wrote, Jerry would edit and enter into the business computer what I was writing. My desire was to be led by The Holy Spirit as I wrote and believe that to have come true. What I didn't realize at the time was how much I was being influenced by these two friends in a collaboration that was preordained by God and guided by The Holy Spirit.

Recently, Jerry shared with me how, as a youth, his great grandfather had shared his faith with him. William Arthur Snidow was born in 1860 and still remembered his father going off the fight in the Civil War. Jerry told me that when he was in college, he took religion courses and what was taught there had little in common with what his great grandfather had taught him. I gave much thought to this and in a later conversation, I asked him if what we had put in my books agreed with what his great grandfather had taught him. His answer was an emphatic YES. How could that not be the case because of our collaboration as I wrote.

It follows that the books with my name on them are actually carrying on what William Arthur Snidow shared with Jerry about 1955. An old time holiness doctrine that has mostly vanished from today's Church. That old time religion was based on living in anticipation and preparation for The Second Coming. It is because of this, several recurring themes appear in my books: Faith in The Promise more than the person - The faith of The First-Century Church; The fulfillment of Jesus' promise to return as The Righteous Judge; and His Promise to rescue the obedient from God's Wrath at The Second Coming.

I must add to this list something new to me - God's Storge Love. This is the affectionate aspect of love that must permeate the other three loves: Eros, Friendship/phileo, and Charity/agape. C.S. Lewis in his book, "The Four Loves", begins with Storge Love/Affectionate Love and makes it about love inside the family. He calls it need love - providing comfort to all of God's Creatures. This mother's milk love must be accompanied with teaching as the family is unified in lifestyle from generation to generation. Being productive and obedient to that lifestyle is the glue that holds the family together living in the hope of His return.

Right after Ephesians 4:11-13, Paul writes this, *"Then we will no longer be infants, tossed back and forth by the waves, and blown here and there by every wind of teaching and by the cunning and craftiness of men in their deceitful scheming. Instead, speaking truth in love, we will in all things grow up into him who is the Head, that is, Christ. From him the whole body, joined and held together by every supporting ligament, grows and builds itself up in love, as each part does its work."*, verses 14-16. This is the very definition of Storge Love and is Truth Love or Tough Love. Speaking truth in love is necessary for His infant children to grow into the maturity of Christ. This is a process that culminates in His Second Coming. At the beginning of this passage, as Paul describes these deceivers, I see a warning for The Family of God that fits today's culture perfectly.

Romans Chapter 8:18-25 provides a unique view of the suffering of sin that leads to the glorious freedom from sin and to Paradise. *"But if we hope for what we do not yet have, we wait for it patiently."*, verse 25. But instead of this hope of resurrection at the last Day, today's culture needs Jesus so that we will go to heaven instantly when we die. Thus we are saved by the free gift of grace and did nothing to earn it and need do nothing to keep it. This is the deception and heartless attitude of today's church, being thankful for a very impersonal gift lacking any element of affection that might make us want to become that new creature. This misses the purity of purpose that Jesus brought into this world and the purity of purpose he brings into our lives.

Producing good fruit is the most important purpose of The Family of God. So much of The Bible is about being fruitful for The Kingdom. And of course obedience to God's instructions is key to producing that good fruit. This is where that elusive relationship and friendship with God begins, not only for the individual, but for the whole culture. An obedient lifestyle is the foundation which produces fruit in keeping with repentance and must be taught from generation to generation. Remember, Jesus cursed the fig tree when it did not produce fruit and it withered and it died.

Abraham was called a friend of God but that friendship has taken a backseat to another friendship, *"You adulterous people, don't you know that friendship with the world is hatred toward God? Anyone who chooses to be a friend of the world becomes an enemy of God."*, James 4:4. The only way to flee the coming wrath is to trust and obey The One who comes to rescue us from that wrath "on that Day".

When we walk with the Lord In the light of His Word
What a glory He sheds on our way! Let us do His good will;
He abides with us still, and with all who will trust and obey.
Then in fellowship sweet We will sit at His feet
or we'll walk by His side in the way; what He says we will do,
where He sends we will go; never fear, only trust and obey.
Trust and obey, for there is no other way
to be happy in Jesus, but to trust and obey.
LIFESTYLE MATTERS!

PART 2: RECLAIMING A CHRISTIAN MORAL COMPASS

Identity Christianity

A Christian identity is not seen in ethnic markers, but in the content of one's character, behavior and lifestyle. The progressive movement in our politics have labeled Christians who believe that America was created to be a Christian Nation and should remain that way as "Christian Nationalists". This group of people have been identified as enemies of America and our Constitution and as such need to be targeted as undesirable. When I enlisted in the Army during Vietnam, I took an oath to "Preserve, protect and defend the Constitution from all enemies, both foreign and domestic." That oath did not have a time stamp on it. The Progressives have labeled the men who created our Constitution, who also had a Christian world view, as enemies of our founding documents. These progressives are therefore domestic enemies of those men who created those documents and founded our country. They pride themselves in rewriting our history and then sabotage any effort to stop them.

The war on Christian ethics can be seen in the progressive's assault on Donald Trump. They have put a target on his back and labeled him as an enemy of our Constitution also. He has said that his success will be in his re-election and this will be his revenge. The A.G. of New York State vowed to prosecute him for a business deal where everyone involved got what they wanted - got paid. She used the power of her office to fine him close to $500 million for doing that successful business deal. In like manner, the D.A. of New York City is trying to put the former president in prison for succeeding in ending a phony story that could have cost him the 2016 election. It looks like continuing these efforts will be just the thing that sends him back to The Oval Office.

What has been revealed in both these cases is that Donald Trump has been the victim of a shake-down of extortion and larceny. All of which has been done to keep him from returning to the White House. The harder they try to find lawlessness in Donald Trump, the more lawless they become. In his impeachments and these trials the best that they can come up with is a couple of phone calls where he was just doing his job as President and making sure all the votes for him were counted in Georgia.

God is using this assault on Donald Trump to reveal who these people are and their lack of A Christian Moral Compass. English preacher John Wesley prophesied that the theology of the Church of England (Calvinism) would lead to lawlessness and the moral decay of that culture. George Washington, his contemporary and others made the point that, "This government would only work for a moral people." No wonder our government seems to be broken. Today, one by one, countries around the world are finding out the truth of George Washington's wisdom and the threat of the heartless immoral religion of the progressive/WOKE agenda.

The success of this new government did not demand that everyone be Christian like it was in England. The nation they created demanded and must be guided by A Christian Moral Compass. Putting the power of government in the hands of the people demanded that they have this morality regardless of whether or not they believed in God. Without that understanding the founders would have just traded one Tierney for another. A Christian Moral Compass had to be taught to each generation to make this new government work.

Reclaiming A Christian Moral Compass in this country is the only means by which the Tierney we see developing in The Federal Government can and will be stopped. The four years of the Biden administration has turned Ukraine and the Middle East into "dumpster fires". Four more years of this agenda will in all probability turn the whole world into one big dumpster fire.

The success or failure of The American Dream is dependent on how we deal with this assault on our Christian values. Understanding how progressives operate both in The Church and in the culture is step one in winning this battle. William Jennings Bryant, famous for the Scopes Monkey Trial, seems to bring the progressive movement in The Church and our national government together. He treated our founding documents and The Gospel/Bible like a buffet, picking and choosing what to believe and how to interpret both. I'm not sure if I'm being fair to him, but it is how progressives operate today. Decoupled from the truth - they lie and deny-deny-deny. Our justice system depends on Christian values from its creation to its enforcement. Without those values, chaos, lawlessness and moral decay will reign which seems to be their goal. Their war on these values is a war on The American Way of Life.

Family Love/Storge Love

The Greek word that best describes the progressive movement is Astorge, translated as a heartless attitude in English. The word astorge appears near the end of Romans Chapter 1. Starting at verse 29, "They have become filled with every kind of wickedness, evil, greed, and depravity. They are full of envy, murder, strife, deceit, and malice. They are gossips, slanderers, God-haters, insolent, arrogant, and boastful; they disobey their parents; they are senseless, faithless, heartless (astorge), ruthless. Although they know God's righteous decree that those who do such things deserve death, they not only do these very things but also approve of those who practice them". This long list describes different things that heartless people do, but one need not do them all to be WOKE - Willfully Overlooking Known Evil.

In several places, Paul writes that those who practice disobedient lifestyles must be put out of The Church. Speaking truth in love, he lets everyone know that those who do such things will not inherit The Kingdom of God. His hope is that this will be a wake-up call for them to repent and make a holy, obedient lifestyle their goal. Then what Peter says in 1Peter 1:8&9 comes true, "Though you have not seen Him, you love Him; and even though you do not see now, you believe in Him and are filled with an inexpressible and glorious joy, for you are receiving (earning... for yourselves) the goal of your faith, the salvation of your souls.", earning...for yourselves - from The Pure Word. Not working for the reward, but working to be worthy of the reward.

The last thing Paul says in Romans 1 may be the most relevant thing for today's church. Those who practice disobedience give permission to those around them to do the same. A Christian Moral Compass must be the main thing to maintain order in the American Culture. Today it has been disconnected from one's own personal holiness and lifestyle in many churches. All of which gives rise to the chaos we see today. When Paul wrote this, the culture was under Roman and Jewish Law. The attempt to take A Christian Moral Compass based on Jewish Law and what Jesus taught out of our culture could be followed by an attempt to replace it with Sharia Law. There is no doubt that the leaders in Iran, and many in America, would love to see this happen.

This also describes those who teach hate, for example, Trump Derangement Syndrome and Hamas teaching their children to hate the Jews. In different ways and to different degrees, this is astorge, a heartless attitude. The Greek word that has the opposite meaning, Storge means affectionate love especially in the family to include The Family of God. Bringing all of this out in this passage indicates that Paul is dealing here with the loss of a Christian Moral Ethic in those to whom he is writing, The Church at Rome. It seems that the progressive movement was alive and well in that church at the very beginning.

Today, progressives are using hatred and false narratives to fundamentally transform America, The Church and The World into a new world order - "One World Order". The useful idiots that are needed for this transformation have the freedom to choose to destroy the very freedom they enjoy here and to destroy this great country. Everything the progressives want in this world will follow this destruction. This collapse is not far off. Everything I have written points to this conclusion. This was not in my head when I started writing, but it is now. I feel very much like God chose me for this task and I hope to hear, at His return, "Well done good and faithful servant."

To Reclaim A Christian Moral Compass we must understand the difference between Agape love and Storge love the opposite of a heartless attitude. Agape love is defined as charity in Scripture. This is why it is so important see salvation as a promised reward at the end of the journey rather than a pure gift, a hand out (salvation full and free), freely given at the moment of belief which brings with it a sense of entitlement. Making the gift of salvation an act of charity - a participation trophy - is one of the reasons that The New Testament Church is dying.

Storge love can be defined as family, affectionate love passed on from generation to generation. The promise of salvation is freely given to all but the actual gift is kept safe in heaven for Jesus' return, reference 1Peter 1:3-5. This makes Storge, tough love the key element which continually builds moral character in the family. It makes us accountable to each other and to God. Living a holy, obedient lifestyle also makes us worthy of the promised reward. Speaking truth in love, it is helpful to see Jesus at His return, calling all of us out of the grave and for those "good and faithful servants", dragging them across the finish line.

This contrast has been put on display, vividly, in today's presidential debate. Donald Trump, his family and others who support him display Christian family values, strong moral character and a work ethic to provide a better life for those who come after them. They build things up; they do not tear things down. For Joe Biden, his family and those who surround him and support him, the opposite is true. All his life, he has damaged everything he claims to love due to greed, lying and selling his soul to the devil, all to win elections and enrich himself and his family. At great personal expense, Donald Trump has given up a life of leisure - leading the way to Make America Great Again. After growing up on the streets of New York, I must say he needed to and has cleaned up his language a great deal. I believe that he is beginning to understand that a renewed emphasis on morality will be needed for the MAGA movement to succeed. "This Government will only work for a moral people."

Freudian Projection

Accusing Donald Trump of having the morals of an ally cat is a reality check for Joe Biden. He has projected on to his opponent the ally cat morals of his son, whom he has called the most decent man he knows and the inverse reality comes true. Joe seems to have made his son Hunter, a convicted felon with his ally cat morals, his most trusted advisor. Hunter's lap-top is revealing the massive amounts of foreign money that came into the family - a crime family with Joe Biden at the top. He then accuses Donald Trump of being a "one-person crime wave". This after democrats spent nearly ten years trying to find a crime in the Trump organization, they have come up with nothing. The irony of this reality is breath-taking and may reveal that Donald Trump is the most decent man Joe Biden has ever met.

It is worth noting here that in a demonstration in Charlottesville, Va. over tearing down confederate statues, Donald Trump, in an attempt to bring order out of chaos, went there and said that there were good people on both sides of this issue. In reality, his statement has revealed that there are some really bad, destructive people on both sides. Twisting The Presidents words here continues to be used by Joe Biden to further the progressive agenda and to tear down America as it was founded. Ironically, President Trump was there trying to deal with a very destructive and divisive issue. Joe Biden, who campaigned on bringing Americans together, continues to use this episode to divide us even further.

Promoting entitlement is a spiritual sickness of greed for power and money done by people without a strong moral ethic. Taking God out of American classrooms was step one in taking biblical morality out of our culture. Anyone who gets in their way will have a target on their back, just like Donald Trump. Imagine what the world would be like without A Cristian Moral Compass. China, North Korea, Iran, Russia and progressives everywhere seem to be coming together in this common cause. Do you think that God did not see this coming? The idea of the earth burning up with fire and brimstone is not new. What is new is a reverential fear that man is causing the problem with global warming and thus replacing a reverential fear of God's wrath. This is evidence of their true agenda.

As Donald Trump's lead in the polls expands, the progressive's rhetoric and descent becomes more revealing adding to his lead and war chest. What Paul saw in The Church at Rome is now vividly on display here in America. "You, therefore, have no excuse, you who pass judgment on someone else, for at whatever point you judge the other, you are condemning yourself, because you who pass judgment do the same things. Now we know that God's judgment against those who do such things is based on truth.", Romans 2:1,2. The threats of more gag orders and imprisonments has been stopped by The Supreme Court. The resulting talk of assassination, the ultimate gag order, causes me to fear for Donald Trump's life.

Signing 12 personal checks while he was in office became 34 felony counts against Donald Trump for paying hush money to help him win the 2016 election. Note: he signed those checks long after the election. Fast-forward, we find Joe Biden, just prior to the 2020 election, getting 51 high ranking government officials to sign a letter to hush-up son Hunter's laptop because it was "Russian disinformation". This was a colossal lie and reveals the length to which they will go to gaslight the American People.

Fast forward to today, we find Joe Biden's A.G. trying to hush-up the audio of Joe's interview with Special Prosecutor Hur's report. They fear that making this recording public will have a dramatic effect on the up-coming election. Hur's report found many instances where Joe Biden could be prosecuted but failed to recommend it. When it comes to hiding things from the American people, Joe's team is the best including hiding the man himself and today, it matters not who heads that team.

The fundamental transformation of America that the Biden-Obama team have promised on occasion seems to be a desire for America to become a third world banana republic - creating crisis after crisis to include locking up those who oppose them. The WOKE policies of the progressive movement under Joe Biden, along with promoting their fear of climate-change, threaten to destabilize governments around the world in like manner. Supporters of Hamas rioting on college campuses chanting "death to America" and threatening to withhold their votes from Joe Biden reveals their agenda - death to America as it was founded.

A Biblical Solution

In Romans Chapter 2, verses 5-8 we find The Gospel Paul preached in a nut shell, "But because of your stubbornness and unrepentant heart, you are storing up wrath against yourself for the day of God's wrath, when his righteous judgment will be revealed. God 'will give to each person according to what he has done.', (Psalms 62:12; Prov. 24:12). To those who by persistence in doing good seek glory, honor and immortality, he will give eternal life. But for those who are self-seeking and who reject the truth and follow evil, there will be wrath and anger." Reading around this, verses 1-16, you will find all you need to know about what losing A Christian Moral Compass looks like.

Here in Romans, Paul is very strongly connecting willful disobedience and immorality to the loose of immortality and the reward of eternal life. This connection is made by Jesus in Matthew 7:21, "Not everyone who says to me 'Lord, Lord,' will enter the kingdom of heaven, but only he who does the will of my father who is in heaven." Verse 23, "Then I will tell them plainly, 'I never knew you. Away from me you evil doers!' " In both of these passages, a holy, obedient lifestyle, God's will for our lives, is the issue and determines our destination. Purity of purpose in the journey starts with A Christian Moral Compass as we live out what Jesus taught.

One thing that is missing with the "I never knew you crowd" is doing the will of the Father. This is the main element in that elusive close, personal relationship with Jesus spoken of so often. A good example of this relationship is in Jesus' interaction with Martha at the tomb of Lazarus. Jesus said to her, "your brother will rise again." Martha answered him, "I know he will rise again in the resurrection at the last day.", John 11:23&24. Read around this and you see what a close relationship with Jesus looks like. But how do we make this real in our own lives by just reading about it in Scripture?

At the end of The Sermon on the mount, Jesus gets to the point of Matthew 7 and the "I never knew you crowd". Doing the will of The Father is at the heart of what Jesus is teaching here. He that hears Jesus' words and puts them into practice is the wise man who builds a rock solid foundation. He who hears Jesus' words and does not put them into practice is the foolish man who chips away at that foundation and turn it into sand.

In The Gospel of John Chapter 14, Jesus gives us a detailed picture of the elements of the relationship between God the Father and mankind that He came to nurture. A close, personal relationship with Jesus has at its center his need to show us the way to that close, personal relationship with the Father. It is here in John 14 that Jesus speaks to the need for obedience as he promises that He and The Father will come and make their home here and dwell with us "on the Day." Jesus uses the pronouns "he and him" referring to those who are obedient which becomes a very personal promise when He indicates it will be a face-to-face encounter at their return, on that Day, reference verses 20-23. Making verse 6 into a series of prepositional phrases reveals this concept. "Jesus answered, 'I am the way to the truth and to the life. No one comes to the father except through me.' ".

This shows that focusing on going to heaven, when we die, is a distraction from achieving that close, personal relationship with God that was present in the beginning. The focus of The Church should be on restoration to paradise, at their return, right here on this earth. God The Father dwelled in harmony with His children in the Garden until they chose to disobey. But in this coming new age, sin and the desire to sin will have been conquered. Choosing to obey is pivotal in having that close, personal relationship with The Father now and forever more. "So Christ was once offered to bear the sins of many; and unto them that look for him shall he appear a second time without (sin nature and) sin unto salvation.", Hebrews 9:28, KJV. "Sin nature and", taken from The Pure Word. Faith in Jesus' promise to return bringing salvation with Him is absolutely the faith that saves.

The growing division and hopelessness we see in America today is a result of the progressive movement's celebration of immorality and must be stopped. God has chosen Donald Trump to be the point of the spear in this effort. The Biden-Obama team and their supporters live in a world mostly devoid of A Christian Moral Compass. God is using Joe Biden's dementia in his speech and his supporter's words to show this assault on those who mostly have A Christian Moral Compass.

There is currently a movement in several states to put The Covenant, The Ten Commandments back into their class rooms. This is being and will be strongly resisted in court and is evidence of the continuing war on A Christian Moral Compass. Make no mistake, this is a war on the American Family and our way of life. The war on Donald Trump, his fortune, his family and his political aspirations is evidence and an important part of their war on the Christ's Church prophesied in Scripture. Seeing their end game for what it is helps me see Donald Trump in this light. Jesus warns us about "Wolves in Sheep's Clothing...you will know them by their fruit." A war on God's Covenant is a war on Christian Morals, a war on family values, a war on The American Way of Life, a war on this country and our founding documents.

The Founding Fathers saying in various way that the government would only work for a moral people was not to cram Christianity down the American People's throat. It was there to establish a moral code of conduct for every American no matter what their station in life or religious belief. And like I wrote earlier from The Sermon on the Mount, it is foolish for anyone to chip away at the foundation of these moral instructions beginning with The Ten Commandments and turning them into sand.

The focus of the war in Israel seems to be turning towards their northern border with Jordan. This is in the area where the battle of Armageddon is prophesied to take place. Many people, including me, feel as though Jesus' Second Coming will be soon. Trying to fit the 42 months of tribulation (Apocalypse - the seventh trumpet and Christ's return) into today's events, I come up with this: Joe Biden's reign begins the first week of January 2021 when the electoral college met, January 6th. Bagram Air Force Base was abandoned 6 months later, the first week of July 2021. The electoral college will vote into office the next president the first week of January 2025, the third anniversary of the January 6th demonstration. This is exactly 42 months after abandoning Afghanistan to the Taliban. These 42 months can be divided into 7 - 6 month segments, each one begins and ends with the anniversary of one of these two events.

It follows that WWIII might break out at the end of Joe Biden's reign, the first week of January 2025. Jesus will come back at this moment, at the last trumpet. There is little doubt that all hell will break loose when the electoral college meets no matter who won on November 5th. It would be very ironic if Donald Trump would be finally elected to his second term at the last trumpet, "in a flash, in the twinkling of an eye, at the last trumpet (trump KJV). For the trumpet will sound, the dead will be raised imperishable and we will all be changed.", 1Cor. 15:52. I believe that God has a great sense of humor even in something as serious as this.

These 42 months are prophesied in the last six verses of The Prophet Daniel and are echoed in Revelation 12:14. Daniel has been proved very accurate in his 70 weeks. Jesus died at the end of the 69th week and we are in a count hold now in The Age of Grace. The start of 70th week ends The Age of Grace and begins the 7-year Tribulation which is divided in half. The blowing of the seventh trumpet happens at the halfway point and announces Jesus' return. This is referred to as Mid-Tribulation and I believe the best understanding of how it all come together.

When I overlay Daniel 12, Ezekeil 39 and Revelation 12 with The last 4 years it becomes clear to me that we are at the end of the first half of The Tribulation. The 1290 days in Daniel are 43 months which includes a leap month added to what should be 1260 days or 42 months. Then come the 1260 days in Revelation or the 42 months of the second half ot The Tribulation. In The King James Version of this accounting we find 15 days and 30 days added for a total of 1335 days with no explanation. It must be that these 30 days are the last 30 days of the 1290 and the 15 days are part of those 30 days. This makes more sense and explains the 1290 days in Daniel. It is wrong to add these 45 days to the 1290 days.

"From the time that the daily sacrifice is abolished and the abomination that causes desolation is set up, there will be 1290 days.", Daniel 12:11. Abandoning Bagram AFB, (July 1, 2021), sets this count in to motion. The first week of January 2025 begins this leap month, 42 months later. Start counting these 15 days on January 6th which then pinpoints January 20th, inauguration day. The events of these 30 days will be at the beginning of "the end of days". There are forces in this country and around the world who will do anything to keep this transfer of power from happening on January 20th. In Daniel 12;8-9, Daniel asks, "My lord, what will the outcome of all this be?" He replied, "Go your way, Daniel, the words are closed up and sealed until the time of the end."

Today, many feel that we are in the time of the end or that it is very near. The conversation that Jesus has with "The Woman at the Well" in John Chapter 4 comes to mind as I try to bring the time of the seventh trumpet into focus for today. Picking up this conversation at John 4:14, Jesus says to the woman, "but, whoever drinks the water I give them will never thirst. Indeed, the water I give them will become in them a spring of water welling up to eternal life." Shortly, Jesus shifts the focus of the conversation to the woman's marital life.

The fountain of water Jesus has just discribed becomes, for me, "The Fountain of Youth". I tease my wife that when Jesus calls us out of the grave to live in His Kingdom forever we will be young again, hopefully, with all the natural desires of our youth. This is the paradise that Jesus promises the thief on the cross and it is the reward that awaits all those who put their trust in Jesus looking forward to His return and this fountain of youth.

The greatest gift Jesus gives to us is The Promise to return and reward us for living a holy, obedient life that pleases Him and The Father. He speaks to us in truth and love. This promise is also the greatest gift that we can pass on to our children and the generations to come. We must also speak truth in love to the whole world, learning and then teaching disciples to practice a holy, obedient lifestyle in anticipation and preparation for Jesus' promised return as The Righteous Judge "on that Day". This is OUR ONLY HOPE.

PART 3: GOD USES WHO HE CHOOSES

I wrote the last bit of part 2 of this book the Saturday morning before Donald Trump was wounded that evening. In the aftermath, I began to see that when that bullet pierced his ear, the whole world saw his 'born again" moment. We now see a changed man - his facial expressions have changed. Unlike he looked in the pictures of him holding a Bible in front of a church across from the White House. I believe it was the evening after his inauguration. Those two moments and those pictures have God's finger prints all over them. In the assassination attempt, people are wondering how this could have even happened. "For we know that in all things God works for the good of those who love him, who have been called according to his purpose.", Romans 8:28.

God can orchestrate any event for any reason and make it serve His purpose. Some see this event as God saving Donald Trump's life when the bullet just missed. It is just as plausible that everything leading up to the event was set in motion by God's design. The phrase "divine appointment" is used to identify such events in people's lives. It is often used to note the moment one comes to belief in Jesus and The Holy Spirit is given sole credit. Seeing this event as a Damascus Road experience is what needs to happen and a life changing moment for Donald Trump. This could become a life changing moment for everyone who loves this country and witnessed this event.

Wondering about the motivation of the snipper is a mystery that may never be known. If it can be linked to the liberal media and their years long assault on Donald Trump, I doubt if that will ever be revealed. What has been revealed is how Donald Trump's speech on January 6th made him guilty of what other people did after he urged them to march peacefully and patriotically to The Capitol. All of the rhetoric and hate speech coming from Joe Biden, Kamala Harris and many others, especially in the media, for the last four years, will never be connected to the snipper. Trump Derangement Syndrome has revealed that twisting the events of J6, their alternative reality, has come back to bite the insurrection crowd. They are as guilty as the snipper!

The Democrats have for nearly ten years called Donald Trump, in one way or another, an existential threat to The American Way of Life. Any unstable person could use these accusations and see killing Donald Trump as a patriotic deed. Recently, many in the liberal media have feared that Donald Trump, if reelected, would have the power and motivation to assassinate his political enemies. The perfect storm we can see unfold that Saturday is not just a series of human blunders by men who seem to have been blinded. It is God's plan unfolding for those who stand firm on Romans 8:28. GOD IS IN CONTROL.

Purity of Purpose

"For the Son of Man came to seek and save what was lost.", Luke 19:10, reveals Jesus' true mission in all that He did and taught. This is at the heart of all that happened at that rally. God setting into motion that event is just another example of His need to reveal His power to save and reveal that to the whole world. The snipper's bullet that found its mark in the spectator who died protecting his family is an example of the purity of God's purpose for those who live for The Kingdom. God, saving Donald Trump's life at that moment, has revealed that same purity of purpose going forward in his life. It is obvious that he sees himself now on a mission from God. That "born again" moment was not about securing his place in heaven, it was about God purifying him for the journey he was already on.

This purity of purpose grows out of having A Christian Moral Compass and wanting that same element to return and dominate our culture. A young man whose psychologist parents taught him - who knows what - do whatever feels good - came to that rally on a mission. He shot at a man who needs to promote Reclaiming A Christian Moral Compass in this country - missed and shot and killed Corey Comperadore who had A Christian Moral Compass. Once again, this government only works for a moral people - that is the imperative and has to be the takeaway here for everyone. Without instilling that morality in our school age children, there will be no immortality for them as with the snipper.

The twenty-year old snipper's formative school years led to him becoming a political activist. There is nothing wrong with this for most kids. But in this case he must have spent those years becoming a "Never Trumper" activist. Influenced by progressive messaging in the news and being taught to hate Trump, this probably consumed him and turned him into an assassin. Hate speech is a very dangerous thing when it is used to promote a political agenda. He wasn't a loose Canon just looking for something to shoot at, he was on a mission.

At about the same time the snipper was getting his secondary education, my oldest grandchild was getting a degree in Criminal Justice at Radford University. There are two things that stand out to me from what she learned: A soft on crime perspective similar to Kamala Harris' and what I see in her agenda and; The CRT movement and blaming white, baby-boomer men for what is wrong in America. This had a very adverse effect on my relationship with my granddaughter at that time and may be at the heart of the progressive's unified assault on Donald Trump. He is a baby-boomer and has become their poster child for what is wrong in America.

In its simplest terms: A snipper, devoid of A Christian Moral Compass, shot to kill a man who will be in a position to promote A Christian Moral Compass to the whole world. But instead, shot and killed a man who by his lifestyle and his actions at that moment, put A Christian Moral Compass on display for the whole world. Corey Comperadore took a bullet meant for Donald Trump as he tried to protect his wife and daughter from the gunfire coming from the left side. Donald Trump survived that same gunfire coming from the left and came up with his fist raised and "FIGHT - FIGHT - FIGHT" on his lips. This is my view and perspective of that moment that made a perfect picture and, I believe, a perfect irony. It will live on in the minds of all those who witnessed that event and should remind all of us of Romans 8:28.

GOD USES WHO HE CHOOSES and HE IS IN CONTROL!

The Faith That Saves

As I try to bring this book to a close, I and many others are mourning the death of my friend Jerry Payne. His picture of him being held by his great-grandfather, is on the front cover of this book. The Faith that William Arthur Snidow shared with young Jerry when He was about 12 was, at its core, his faith in Christ's Second Coming. With their influence in my life and my writing, I found the perfect definition of this faith somewhat hidden in Hebrews 11. Connecting verses 1,2,39,40, "Now faith is being sure what we hope for and certain of what we do not (yet) see. This (faith) is what the ancients were commended for…These were all commended for their faith, yet none of them received what had been promised. God had planned something better for us so that only together with us would they be made perfect."

In Verse 11:6, the writer of Hebrews makes this faith in the promise a sure part of our reward and by extension the ancient's reward. "And without (this) faith it is impossible to please God, because anyone who comes to him must believe that he exists and that he rewards those who earnestly seek him." We are perfected in this faith and the ancients are perfected by our faith. Jerry lived this deep faith and by sharing it with me as I wrote, it has become a window into a world of simple faith and holy living as best as our forefathers could model for us.

Jesus tells us about a faith that is a mile wide and an inch deep compared to a faith that is in inch wide and a mile deep. "Enter through the narrow gate. For wide is the gate and broad is the road that leads to destruction, and many enter through it. But small is the gait and narrow is the road that leads to life, and only a few find it." This is the deep faith that my friend Jerry lived and poured into my life coming from his great-grandfather.

This faith that perfects us and the ancients becomes for us, like Abraham, our righteousness. When we appear before God at Judgment we will all be justified by this faith and clothed in His Righteousness. This faith then in turn becomes our wedding clothes. Jews and Christians alike are united in waiting for this "Soon Coming King" - The Bridegroom. The Jews wanted a warrior king to rescue them from the Romans, but instead, got The Suffering Servant King. When Jesus comes again He will be more like that warrior king - the Righteous Judge rescuing the obedient as God's wrath is poured out on the disobedient.

The Parable of The Ten Virgins paints a prefect picture of this event and "A Watch Party Gospel". The Wise Virgins lived in anticipation and preparation for The Bridegroom's return - The Foolish Virgins did not and were locked out. "But he replied, 'I tell you the truth, I don't know you.' 'Therefore keep watch, because you don't know the day or the hour.', Matthew 25:12,13.

"Blessed are the pure in heart, for they will see God.", Matthew 5:8.

"I delight greatly in my Lord; my soul rejoices in my God.

For He has clothed me with garments of salvation

and arrayed me in a robe of righteousness,

as a bridegroom adorns his head like a priest,
and a bride adorns herself with her jewels.", Isaiah 61:10.

"When He shall come with trumpet sound, oh may I then in him be found - dressed in His righteousness alone, faultless before the throne.", Solid Rock.

Paul gives us the perfect application of "this faith in the promise" in 2Timothy 4: 6-8, "For I am already being poured out like a drink offering, and the time has come for my departure. I have fought the good fight, I have finished the race, I have kept the faith. Now there is in store for me a crown of righteousness, which the Lord, the righteous Judge, will award to me on that day - and not only to me, but also to all who have longed for his appearing." This is The Faith that will save us all. Jerry was not perfect and neither are we, but for those like Jerry who aspire to that perfection - purity of purpose, they will be called out of the grave by Jesus, on that Day, and dragged across that finish line into Paradise. We are all called to live a holy, obedient lifestyle in anticipation and preparation for the return of Jesus as The Righteous Judge.

The writer of Hebrews draws a perfect picture of the elements of Jesus' life and faith in His Father which in turn becomes a perfect example for us to follow. "During the days of Jesus' life on earth, he offered up prayers and patitions with loud cries and tears to the one who could save him from death, and he was heard because of his reverent submission. Although he was a son, he learned obedience from what he suffered and, once made perfect, he became the source of eternal salvation for all who obey him...". Hebrews 5:7-9 NIV. By example, Jesus' obedience made Him one with the Father and in turn, our obedience becomes our atonement and perfects us in The Faith That Saves.

Jesus' return to Paradise and to The Father depended on His obedience to the will of The Father. Jesus' instruction in

Matthew 7:21 then becomes key to His and our return to Paradise, "Not everyone who says to me, 'Lord, Lord,' will enter the kingdom of heaven, but only he who does the will of my Father who is in heaven." What Jesus is teaching and preaching here is a very tall order. The reality of Jesus' point here is that the deeds of the "I never knew you crowd" did not line up with the will of His Father. When He adds to this The Wise and Foolish Builders, it becomes a demand for our obedience to the will of The Father and The Faith and hope in The Promise.

THIS IS OUR ONLY HOPE

THE BLESSED HOPE OF JESUS' RETURN.

AUTHOR BIOGRAPHY

Tom and Shirley live at Providence Farm in Bedford County, Virginia. They met and got married five years ago, and are turning eighty this year. About ten years ago, Tom felt a calling to write about his discontent with The Church that he loves. He feels like The Holy Spirit has led him to three very important conclusions, among others. First, The Church has focused on marketing salvation for centuries when it should be focused on living a holy life that leads to the awarding of salvation at Jesus Christ's Second Coming. Second, that commitment and genuine faith begin this journey, and that an obedient lifestyle is the foundation on which the hope of eternal life rests. Jesus comes back to rescue us from The Coming Wrath when God's Wrath is poured out on the disobedient at Final Judgment. And third, The Woke element that wants to destroy our country, as it was founded, is being taught in our universities by those who teach our children in our schools and by those who preach to us and teach us in our churches.

www.ingramcontent.com/pod-product-compliance
Lightning Source LLC
LaVergne TN
LVHW010601070526
838199LV00063BA/5030